Abridged Therapeutics

W.H. SCHÜSSLER

Contents

ABRIDGED THERAPEUTICS

BY

W.H. SCHÜSSLER

PREFACE TO THE NINTH EDITION.

THE short space of time which has elapsed between the issue of the eighth and the present edition has not permitted me to gather many-new experiences. All I can offer my readers are some new special Indications.

DR. SCHÜSSLER.
OLDENBURD, *July* 1882.

PREFACE TO THE THIRD EDITION.

I PRESENT my little work in the Third Edition to the public, after having added several Indications, and having completely re-written it.

The First and the Second Editions were so quickly out of print that I may hope the present one will meet the kindly reception of its predecessors.

As every innovation gains by opposition, it is a source of satisfaction to me that some opponents have appeared against my Therapeutics. The views of these critics the reader will find in the part entitled "Refutation of some Objections."

OLDENBURG *May* 1876.

TRANSLATOR'S PREFACE.

WITH Dr. Schüssler's permission I have undertaken the translation of this method of treating disease by means of triturated Tissue Salts,—Constitutional Tonics, which tend to restore the lost or disturbed proper balance of Cell Salts. Its publication in English will, I hope, make it known to many to whom otherwise it might be unavailable.

Biology, Cellular Pathology, Spectrum Analysis, Minute Anatomy, Analytical Chemistry, and such kindred Sciences, have furnished a field of research to this German physician. Professional skill and science combined, have thus led to the elucidation of this new system of Therapeutics.

A General and Therapeutical Index and a Reference Table have been arranged and added by me to the original; the former to give a resumé of diseases which are histo-pathologically alike, and require such remedy as is mentioned at the head of each group.

M.D.W.
DUNDEE, 1880.

INTRODUCTION.

MOLESCHOTT, Professor of Physiology at the University of Rome, says in his work on *"Vital Circulation":* (Kreislauf des Lebens).

"The structure and vitality of the organs depend upon the presence of the necessary quantities of the inorganic constituents."

"On this fact is based the great estimation in which of late years the subject of the relative proportions of the inorganic substances to the individual parts of the body has been held."

"This estimation neither proudly despises any fact, nor fosters, on the other hand, futile hopes; but promises both to Agriculture and Medicine a brilliant future."

"In the face of such positive facts, it can no longer be denied that the substances which remain after incineration or combustion of the tissues—the ashes—are as important and essential to the inner composition, and consequently to the 'form-giving' and 'kind-determining' basis of the tissues, as those substances which are volatilized during combustion."

"A glue-furnishing base and bone-earth are essential constituents of bone. Without either there can be no true bone; so also there can be no cartilage without cartilagesalt; nor blood without iron; nor saliva without Potassium chloride."

"Of earth and air man is made. The activity of the vegetable kingdom called him into life; and in death he returns to air and ashes, that plant-life may in new forms develop new powers."

These words of Moleschott induced me to make a study of the physiologico-chemical effects of the inorganic substances of the human organism.

In consequence of this study, begun nine years ago, there arose a system of what may be called Bio-chemic Therapeutics; a system founded on well-ascertained facts concerning the Chemistry of the Tissues.

"THE CONSTITUENT PARTS OF THE HUMAN ORGANISM."

BLOOD consists of *water, sugar, fat, albuminous substances,* besides common salt, Potassium chloride, Calcium fluoride, Silica, Iron[1], Lime, Magnesia, Soda, and Potash; the latter are combined with either Phosphoric acid or Carbonic acid.

In the blood-plasma the Sodium salts predominate, and in the blood-corpuscles the Potash salts.

Sugar, fat, and the albuminous substances, are the so-called organic components; water and the above-named salts are the inorganic components of the blood.

Sugar and fat are composed of carbon, hydrogen, and oxygen.

Albumen consists of carbon, hydrogen, oxygen, nitrogen, and sulphur.

The blood contains the material for all the tissues of the body. By means of the capillaries (channels delicate as hairs) the arteries are connected with the veins. Through the walls of the capillaries a portion of the blood-liquid transudes con-

---

1 Manganese is not always present; therefore, as far as concerns cell-formation, it may be considered an insignificant constituent of the blood.

tinually into the surrounding tissues (transosmose). In the transuded liquid arise little granules: and these unite to form germs from which cells are developed. These cells-unite, and thus tissues arise,—muscles and tendons, cartilage and bone, brain and nerves, connective-tissue, skin, hair, and nails,—in short, every part of the organism.

In the formation of the tissue-cells the salts absolutely determine the kind of cell. The organic substances form the basis of the cells.

The inorganic substances of nerve and brain cells are: *Magnesium phosphate, Potassium phosphate, Sodium,* and *Iron.* The same salts, along 'with *Potassium chloride,* are met with in muscle-cells. Again, the specific substance of the connective-tissue cells is *Silica;* and of the elastic cells *Calcium fluoride* Of these salts *Magnesium phosphate, Potassium phosphate,* and *Calcium fluoride* are contained in the bones. The bone cells are distinguished by the preponderance in their constitution of *Phosphate of Lime;* but it is also found in minute quantities in muscle, nerve, brain, and connective-tissue cells.

Common salt (Sodium chloride), which occurs in all solid and fluid parts of the organism, is the specific inorganic constituent of cartilage and mucus-cells. The hairs and the crystalline lens contain also iron amongst other inorganic substances.

The CARBONATES, according to Moleschott, are of no importance in cell formation.

The oxygen of the air, after being inhaled, enters the blood and the tissues, causing a transformation of those organic substances which are necessary for the composition of the new cells. The products of the metamorphosis are: muscle substance, nerve substance, connective-tissue substance (glue-furnishing substance), and, lastly, mucus substance. Each of these substances is the basis of a particular group of cells; muscle substance forms the basis of muscle cells, nerve substance of nerve cells, and so on. With these substances the above-mentioned special cell-salts unite by means of their chemical affinity, and thus new cells are formed.

While the formation of new cells is going on, the old cells are being destroyed by the action of oxygen. The organic substances which form the basis of these cells undergo a process of oxidation or combustion. In consequence of this process, the cells themselves are destroyed.

Through the combustion of the organic substances arise: Urea, Uric acid, Sulphuric acid, Phosphoric acid, Lactic acid, Carbonic acid, and water. There are, doubtless, several intermediate grades, as, for instance, uric oxide, acetic acid, butyric acid, etc., but with these we are not concerned in this system of Therapeutics.

Urea, uric acid, and sulphuric acid, are produced by the oxidation of the albuminous substances. Phosphoric acid is produced by the combustion of the so-called yolk-fat (Dotterfett), which contains phosphorus. Yolk-fat is found in the nerves, brain, spinal chord, and blood corpuscles.

Sugar turns into lactic acid, and the lactic acid in its turn is decomposed into carbonic acid and water.

Sulphuric and phosphoric acids unite with the bases of the carbonates, and carbonic acid is given off. In this way sulphates and phosphates are produced.

Uric acid unites with sodium, and becomes sodium urate, which, being of no use in the economy of the body, has to be eliminated. When this salt accumulates about the joints,. it gives rise to gout.

The *Sodium sulphate* effects the elimination of water arising from the oxidation of the organic substances of the body.

Sodium sulphate (Glaubersalt) and *Sodium chloride,* or common salt, act in opposite ways. Whilst the *Sodium sulphate* effects the elimination from the tissues of the water above referred to, *Sodium chloride,* on the other hand, enters. with water, etc., from the plasma (blood liquid), into the tissues. This latter process takes place so that each tissue may receive its requisite amount of moisture.

By the presence of the *Sodium phosphate* the lactic acid is decomposed into carbonic acid and water. This salt has the power of holding carbonic acid in combination, in the proportion of two parts of carbonic acid to one of phosphoric acid. It also carries the carbonic acid, which it has absorbed, to the lungs. Here it is acted upon by the inhaled oxygen, and the carbonic acid, being only loosely held by the *Sodium phosphate,* is set free. The carbonic acid is then exhaled, and exchanged for oxygen.

The final products of the combustion of the organic substances are: urea, carbonic acid, and water. These products leave the tissues along with the salts which have been set free, giving place to those organic substances which have not yet reached so high a degree of oxidation to allow these also to undergo the final metamorphosis.

The products of this Retrograde Metamorphosis are removed from the system by means of the lymphatics, the connective-tissue, and the veins. They are carried to the gall-bladder, to the lungs, to the kidneys, the bladder, and the skin, and are eliminated from the organism together with the urine, perspiration, fæces, etc.

Concerning the important function of connective-tissue (connective substance) Moleschott thus expresses himself:—"It is one of the "grandest conquests of modern times, to which Virchow and Von Recklinghausen have paved "the way, that this connective substance has been elevated from the indifferent and secondary position formerly allotted to it, to one of fertile activity hitherto unsuspected. That "which was formerly considered simply as a filling-in, or protecting covering, now appears as the bed [nidus] of the most minute sapstreamlets of blood to the tissues, and from them back to the blood-vessels; and, at "the same time, as one of the most important breeding-spots pf young cells, which are "capable of rising out of the undeveloped youthful "forms into the most characteristic formations "of the body."

An individual is in a state of health when the formation of new cells, and the destruction of the old ones, as well as the removal of useless substances, proceed normally; when the blood receives from the food, by the process of digestion, compensation for the losses which it sustains by the giving off of nutriment to the tissues, and in the tissues the nutriment is supplied in the required quantities, and in the proper places, and when no disturbance takes place in the movement of the molecules. A disturbance in the molecular movements of any of the inorganic salts of a tissue produces a disease. For the healing or cure of such, the smallest dose of the identical inorganic substance suffices, because the molecules of that substance, administered as medicine, fill up the gap in the chain of molecules of that particular cell or tissue salt.

The value of minute doses may be seen from the following words of Professor Valentin, the well-known Physiologist:—"Nature works "everywhere with immense numbers of "infinitely small magnitudes of homogenous "structure or otherwise, which can only be "perceived by our comparatively dull organs of "sense when presented to them in finite "masses. The smallest image which our "eye can perceive is produced by millions of "waves of light. A grain of salt which we can "scarcely taste contains millions of groups of "atoms which no human eye will ever discern."

By means of Spectrum analysis, minute particles can be distinguished, which may be compared in magnitude to molecules of my sixth or seventh centesimal saccharated trituration. Professors Kirchhoff and Bunsen[2] took three milligrammes of saccharated **Sodium chloride,** which was blown into the air of a room containing sixty cubic mètres of air. In a few minutes Sodium lines appeared in a flame standing at a considerable distance, which could be distinguished by the unaided eye.

The organic substances and the inorganic salts which are taken into the body as *food* must correspond in quantity to the waste or change of substance; but when administered *medicinally,* only the smallest doses of these salts are requisite. For instance, common salt must be put into food in large or ponderable quantities; but for the cure of certain definite diseases which have arisen notwithstanding the daily use of food seasoned with salt, it must be taken only in minute doses.

How can such a cure be explained? The case is in all probability thus: Through irritation, over stimulation, a certain tissue has lost its molecules of common salt. In consequence of this, that portion of tissue is so changed that it is no longer able to absorb out of the plasma new molecules of salt. The requisite molecules must, therefore, be introduced by some other means.

The molecules of a minimum dose of common salt[3], given as medicine, reach the neurilemma (nerve-sheaths) of those branches of the Sympathetic which ramify through the mucous membrane of the mouth and the upper part to the throat. In this way they proceed to the nearest ganglia (nerve-centres), and from there

2   Kirchhoff and Bunsen's Memoir of analysis by spectrum Observations.—***Philosophical Magazine,*** vol. XX.

3   Spectrum Analysis has opened a new field of truth, showing matter to be capable of division to an extent of which we could form no comprehension. While speaking of the action of molecules of a minimum dose, a statement by Darwin is subjoined, referring to much more minute quantities than those used by Dr. Schüssler. He says in his work on Insectivorous Plants:—"It is an astonishing fact, on which I will not here enlarge, that so inconceivably minute a quantity as one 20,000,000th of a grain of ammonia phosphate should induce some changes in a gland, sufficient to cause a motor impulse to be sent down the whole length of the tentacle; this impulse 'exciting movements through an angle of about 180°."

they pass by the same path, i.e., the ducts of the connective-tissue sheaths of other branches of the Sympathetic, into the diseased tissue. The molecules of a minimum (minutest) dose of common salt thus reach their destination by a route different from that through the stomach, intestines, and blood-vessels. The same mode of locomotion naturally applies also to the molecules of the other cell salts which are given for curative purposes.

When the said portion of tissue has acquired its former healthy condition through this supply of molecules, it possesses again the capability of absorbing *from the plasma* particles of common salt, or any other cell salt.

The presence of a dose of common salt, unattenuated, can be perceived by the nerves of taste (Glossopharyngeus and lingualis). To produce this, it is only necessary that the ends of these nerves be touched by the common salt. It is, however, questionable if the salt in a crude, non-attenuated condition can enter, or can be taken up by the ducts of the neurilemma which envelop the branches of the Sympathetic. It seems probable that these narrow canals can only take up the delicately fine attenuated molecules of *Sodium chloride* and the other tissue salts, when set free by a special process of trituration.

It may not be out of place here to quote some words of Professor Huxley on "Cellular Pathology," from his Address-at the International Medical Congress, London, 1881.

PROFESSOR HUXLEY ON THE CONNECTION OF THE BIOLOGICAL

SCIENCES WITH MEDICINE.

"I trust I have not been mistaken in supposing that am attempt to give a brief sketch of the steps by which a philosophical necessity has become a historical reality may not be devoid of interest, possibly of instruction, to the members of this great Congress, profoundly interested as all are in the scientific development of medicine."

"The greatest physiological and pathological work of the seventeenth century, Borelli's treatise 'De motu animalium,' is, to all intents and purposes, a development of Descartes" fundamental conception; and the same may be said of the physiology and pathology of Boerhaave[4], whose authority dominated in the medical world of the first half of the eighteenth century.

"With the origin of modern, chemistry, and of electrical science, in the latter half of the eighteenth century, aid in the analysis of the phenomena of life, of which Descartes could not have dreamed, were offered to the physiologist. And the greater part of the gigantic progress which has been made in the present century is a justification of the prevision of Descartes. For it consists, especially, in a more and more complete resolution of the grosser organs of the living body into physico-chemical mechanisms. * * 'To apply the physical sciences to physiology is to explain the phenomena of living bodies by the laws of inert bodies.' * * * It is not too much to say that one half of a modern textbook of physiology consists of applied physics and chemistry; and that it is exactly in the exploration of the phenomena of sensibility and contractility that physics and chemistry have exerted the most potent influence. * * 'All animals,' says Bichat, 'are assemblages of different organs, each of which performs its functions and concurs, after its fashion, in the preservation of the whole. They are so many special machines in the general machine which constitutes the individual. But each of these special machines is itself compounded of many tissues of very different natures, which in truth constitute the elements of those organs.'[5] (*l.c.* lxxxiv.) 'The conception of a proper vitality is applicable only to these simple tissues, and not to the organs themselves.' (*l.c.* lxxxiv.)

"And Bichat proceeds to make the obvious application of this doctrine of synthetic life, if I may so call it, to pathology. Since diseases are only alterations of vital properties, and the properties of each tissue are distinct from those of the rest, it is evident that the diseases of each tissue must be different from those of the rest Therefore, in any organ composed of different tissues, one may be diseased and the other remain healthy; and this is what happens in most oases. (*l.c.* lxxxv.) * * In a spirit of true prophecy, Bichat says, 'we have arrived at an epoch, in which pathological anatomy should start afresh.' For as the analysis of the organs had led him to the tissues as the physiological units of the organism; so, in a succeeding-generation, the analysis of the tissues led to the cell as the physiological element of the tissues.* *

---

4   whose lineal descendant is Professor Moleschott, author of "Kreislauf des Lebens," Senator of Rome.

5   Anatomie Générale.

* * In fact, the body is a machine of the nature of an army, not of that of a watch, or of a hydraulic apparatus. Of this-army, each cell is a soldier, an organ a brigade, the central nervous system head-quarters and field telegraph, the alimentary and circulatory system the commissariat. Losses-are made good by recruits born in camp, and the life of the individual is a campaign, conducted successfully for a number of years, but with certain defeat in the long run. * * * Hence the establishment of the cell theory, in normal biology, was swiftly followed by a 'cellular pathology,' as its logical counterpart. I need not remind you how great an instrument of investigation this doctrine has proved in the hands of the man of genius[6], to whom its development is due. * * Henceforward, as it appears to me, the connection of medicine with the biological sciences is clearly defined. Pure pathology is that branch of biology which defines the particular perturbation of cell life, or of the co-ordinative machinery, or of both, on which the-phenomena of disease depend. * * * Those who are-conversant with the present state of biology will hardly hesitate to admit that the conception of the life of one of the higher animals as the summation of the lives of a cell aggregate, brought into harmonious action by a co-ordinative machinery formed by some of these cells, constitutes a permanent acquisition of physiological science. * * * There are some * * who look, with as little favour as Bichat did, upon any attempt to apply the principles and the methods of physics and chemistry to the investigation of the vital processes of growth, metabolism, and contractility: they stand upon the ancient ways.

"Others, on the contrary, supported by a robust faith in the universal applicability of the principles laid down by Descartes, and seeing that the actions called 'vital' are, so far as we have any means of knowing, nothing but changes of place of particles of matter, look to molecular physics to achieve the analysis of the living protoplasm itself into a molecular mechanism. If there is any truth in the received doctrines of physics, that contrast between living and inert matter, on which Bichat lays so much stress, does not exist. In nature, nothing is at rest, nothing is amorphous; the simplest particle of that which men in their blindness are pleased to call 'brute matter' is a vast aggregate of molelcular mechanisms, performing complicated movements of immense rapidity and sensitively adjusting themselves to every change in the surrounding world. * * * * Living matter differs from other matter in

---

6 Virchow.

degree and not in kind; the microcosm repeats the macrocosm; and one chain of causation connects the nebulous original of suns and planetary systems with the protoplasmic foundation of life and organisation.

"From this point of view, pathology is the analogue of the theory of perturbations in astronomy; and therapeutics resolves itself into the discovery of the means by which a system of forces competent to eliminate any given perturbation may be introduced into the economy. And, as pathology bases itself upon normal physiology, so therapeutics rests upon pharmacology; which is, strictly speaking, a part of the great biological topic of the influence of conditions on the living organism, and has no scientific foundation apart from physiology. * * * * It will, in short, become possible to introduce into the economy a molecular mechanism which, like a very cunningly contrived torpedo, shall find its way to some particular group of living elements, and cause an explosion [i.e., absorption and molecular motion] among them, leaving the rest untouched.

"The search for the explanation of diseased states in modified cell life; the discovery of the important part played by parasitic organisms in the ætiology of disease; the elucidation of the action of medicaments by the methods and the data of experimental physiology; appear to me to be the greatest steps which have ever been made towards the establishment of medicine on a scientific basis. I need hardly say they could not have been made except for the advance of normal biology."

The most famous scientist in this country advances suggestions arrived at from his point of view, as is seen by the above, which are in singular agreement with Dr. Schüssler's views and experiences on the subject of scientific medicine.

Biology shows Biochemistry to be a science. The practical counterpart of the abstract science of Cellular Pathology is formed by "Cellular Therapeutics," or the system of introducing molecular cell-salts. The one, indeed, is the forerunner of the other; the former science investigating the morbid states of tissue-cells; the latter, a system by which the natural action or force—fixed by a law of chemical affinity—of any of the inorganic constituents is systematically employed to eliminate any given disease or perturbation from any of the tissue cells by means of molecules' of special adequate magnitude, these setting up molecular motion and equilibrium of balance in the economy of the cells. But only the non-functional tissue cells are acted upon, leaving the rest untouched! In health restored, the physiological laws are suffered to resume their normal course. Law is law, and in Nature unalterable. If man is not the casual production or conjunction of atoms, one may not pass by this wondrous phenomenon which he presents, without acknowledging that this finely wrought composition of organic and inorganic atoms is regulated by a universal law, the teachings of which are far-reaching. By them we arrive by induction at the grand science of "Cellular Therapeutics." Biochemic treatment is the outcome of the teachings of Biology and those sciences which of late years have disclosed Nature's ways and footsteps, by aid of the microscope and spectroscope.

Let every medical man, every student, test this law, and conscientiously apply the molecular tissue cell-salts under given abnormal conditions as indicated, and he will not fail to attain good results. The action by chemical affinity of these triturated molecules of cell salts is certain, because fixed by that law. Close observation of little things is the secret of true science. None who watch the wonderful results in Nature from infinitely minute causes will doubt the power of little things. Little bits of experiences gathered up carefully and arranged systematically make up the store of our knowledge.

Surely those scientists who do not hail so great an advent as the opening up of "Cellular Therapeutics," truly scientific medicine, do not comprehend the deep meaning of their own teachings in this direction, the possibility and rationale of a defined general Law of Cure on these lines. Under the advance of Histology, Analytical Chemistry, Cellular Pathology, etc., it has become possible to group the tissues by their special constitution of definite organic and inorganic substances. Consequently, to apply to each kind of tissue its own general, definite, and peculiar cell salt, according to its requirements in disease.

The promoters of the sister sciences of medicine have made it possible for the physician in future to ***depend*** on the method of operation of his medicines in the living organism, when these are skilfully selected and scientifically applied. By the distinctive symptoms he is guided in his choice of the ***particular*** cell salts required—the immense varieties and complications of morbid states, offering vast scope for exact medical practice, wherewith to build up the great pyramid of scientific medicine of this advanced era.

The Biochemic treatment of disease must not be confounded with Homœopathy, where the whole system rests on a mystic law of "Similia" and symptomatology, where true pathology has no place, and the exact action of the remedy is a mystery, though some would fain try to cloak Homœopathy with this mantle of scientific medicine. Br Schüssler is not a Homœopathy. His new discovery of remedies owes its development, in the first instance, to Biology and its Cell-theory; and in the second, to Cellular Pathology, of which the necessary and natural counterparts are Cellular Therapeutics or Biochemic Treatment of Disease.

THE TRANSLATOR.

Refutation of Some Objections.

DIFFERENT objections have been urged by physicians, who have arraigned my *Abbreviated System of Therapeutics* before the bar of their judgment, and which I now take occasion to refute.

The late Dr. Constantine Hering, of Philadelphia, who informed the American medical profession of the tenor of my therapeutical system in a pamphlet entitled *"The Twelve Tissue Remedies,"* is of the opinion that I should also have embraced carbon and nitrogen among my therapeutical agents. It is, however, well known that neither carbon alone, nor nitrogen alone, enter into the composition of tissue-cells. Carbon and nitrogen are integral parts of the organic substances which form the organic basis of cells. The organic substances are only influenced by inhaled oxygen, and by the inorganic salts. Nitrogen and carbon, therefore, remain useless as therapeutical agents.

If, in the animal organism, nitrogen should, or could, be wanting, then albuminous substances would be wanting, of which nitrogen is an integral part. Albuminous substances can only be introduced into the body by means of food.

Dr. Hering, also, misses the organic acids in my system of therapeutics. How the organic acids, lactic acid and uric acid, are produced, is already noticed under the heading of "Production of Acids," page 16.—No agricultural chemist would think of giving to a sickly vine the organic acids of the grape, because he knows that an inorganic salt (Potassium carbonate) will be the proper remedy.

Only indistinct conceptions of the chemico-physiological processes of the animal organism could have induced Dr. H. to raise such objections.

Dr. H. further insists that spectroscopic analysis would, in course of time, discover several other as yet unknown substances in the tissues of the human body, which would have to be incorporated among the factors of the tissue-therapeutics.

This assertion would seem as intended, in fact, to render the completeness of my therapeutics unattainable for a long time to come.

If, indeed, spectrum analysis could yet discover substances which do contribute to the formation of tissues, such substances would, of course, have to be incorporated among the agents of the tissue-therapeutics.

The inorganic cell-salts already known are, however, able to perform, directly or indirectly, all the functions of the organism.

Another critic insists that there cannot be a strictly defined system of therapeutics applicable to all parts of the world, since each quarter of the globe had its peculiar diseases. To this I must reply that it is not a question of medical nomenclature; but rather that, in a system of tissue-therapeutics, it is only tissues and their functional disturbances which are to be taken into consideration.

If an Ethiopian has muscles, he certainly has ***Potassium chloride, Magnesium phosphate,*** and ***Iron*** in them. A disturbance of the molecules of ***Magnesium phosphate*** in the muscles of an Ethiopian will produce the same phenomena as in those of a European.

The same critic thinks that all diseases might be cured with oxygen, carbon, nitrogen, and hydrogen, better than with my proposed twelve inorganic tissue-salts. These four elements may, perhaps, suffice in the hands of a necromancer, but they would certainly leave a physician in the lurch.

A third opponent, Dr. von Grauvogel of Munich, has been so warped by his persecuting zeal as to fail to notice the contradictions in which he is involved by his own statements.

He says that, with local pathology and local therapeutics, no lasting good is accomplished; that disease is not confined to any one part of the organism, but that the whole organism is, in fact, the disease. Even tumours, apparently isolated, could thus be understood. So he speaks, and, in spite of it, treats chondroma with silica, because this substance is contained in the bones. This, surely, is local therapeutics. It cannot be doubted, however, according to my way of thinking, that local therapeutics are correct. If one has dissipated irritation-hyperæmia by its appropriate remedy, the symptoms dependent upon it—pain, fever, general malaise—have disappeared. If, in consequence of an irritation-hyperæmia, an exudation has taken place, again local treatment is required in order to get rid of the exudation, and, after its removal, the secondary symptoms cease.

If, as Dr. von G. asserts, the whole organism is the disease, then death must, of necessity, be the result of every illness. On page 38 of his book, speaking of the Law of Similars, he says, "From these propositions it follows that the curability or incurability of disease does not shape its course according to its intensity merely; but principally according to the quality, quantity, and relation of the remaining healthy parts." If, according to Dr. von G., the whole organism is the disease, how can there be any talk of "remaining healthy parts?"

Dr. von G. further says that, according to Gorup Besanez, the physiological localities of the chemical constituents of the body were, on the whole, yet unknown, therefore a physiological principle could not be perfected. If Dr. von G. shares the views of Besanez, what then induces him to adopt his expression, "relation of Silica to the bones," and consequently to use Silica as a remedy in chondroma and rachitis?

"All means of nourishment are also means of function," says Dr. von G. Soon after he thus expresses himself: "Therefore, one can speak of substances as means of function, only so far as they are not constituent parts of the body."

How does that harmonise?

Dr. von G.'s hobby horse, "Logic," seems to be not so well ridden by him as he himself believes.

That all inorganic ***means of nutrition*** are, at the same time ***means of function,*** is a proposition which I endorse. It never occurred to me to undertake for practical purposes a definite division of the cell-salts into means of function and of building material. I call them building material, in so far as they occupy a place in the organic basis of the cells; and means of function, in respect of their chemico-physiological action.

Dr. von G. says, "Schüssler demands that facts should shape themselves according to his. theories." Not at all, honoured sir! My therapeutical system has arisen between theory and practice, constantly and mutually controlling and correcting each other.

Not I, but Dr. von G., demands that facts should shape themselves according to his ideas. To cure chancre he uses Glauber's salt, but the disease steadily resists. This, at least, is averred by physicians who have made similar experiments.

Dr. von G., after a long *raisonnement* about means of adaptation, imbibition, effusion, etc., insists that there can only be a system of molelcular— not cellular— therapeutics. Despite Dr. von G.'s disquisition, I shall retain the term Cellular Therapeutics, since I consider it as more correct.

For instance, you supply iron molecules to the blood-cells needing iron; you render a service to the respective cells, and such service carried out for the benefit of these cells may, without solecism, be termed a system of cellular therapeutics. If one causes, by therapeutical means, iron molecules to enter the cells through the molecular interstices of the blood-cell membrane, the service is rendered not to the iron molecules, but to the cells. To dispute whether one should call it a system of cellular—or molecular—therapeutics, is simply a piece of ridiculous pedantry.

To the critics who have hitherto arisen against me, I quote the words of Voltaire, in La Pucelle d'Orléans:—

"Censeurs savants, je vous estime tous; Je connais mes défauts mieux que vous."

CHARACTERISTICS OF THE INORGANIC TISSUE-SALTS.

Ferric Phosphate.

IRON is a constituent of the blood-corpuscles, and of the muscle-cells, etc. When the equilibrium of the iron molecules in the muscular fibres is disturbed, the latter become relaxed. When such a disturbance of proper balance takes place in the circular fibres of the blood-vessels, the vessels enlarge, and a blood-accumulation arises in the vascular parts (capillaries) so affected. When, in consequence of an increased pressure of blood, a rupture of the walls of the blood-vessels ensues, bleeding [hæmorrhage] will follow.

When the muscles of the intestinal villi [absorbants] suffer a functional disturbance of their iron molecules, loose evacuations will follow.

When, in consequence of a molecular disturbance of the proper balance of the iron, the muscular fibres of the intestinal walls become weakened, then the vermicular action of the intestines proceeds with less activity, and gives rise to a tendency to constipation.

Iron molecules, therapeutically employed, allay the pathological functional disturbance.

Whilst iron restores to their normal condition the blood-vessels, enlarged by disease, it dispels the irritation-hyperæmia [local excess of blood], which is the cause of the first stage of all inflammations.

Hyperæmia dependent upon a mechanical injury is cured by iron; and fresh non-suppurating wounds are quickly healed by this remedy.

Iron and the iron salts possess the property of attracting oxygen. In this fact consists their utility to the respective tissue-cells. I use the **Ferric phosphate** or phosphate of iron.

Upon my recommendation several farmers have given Ferric phosphate, with uniform success, to sows possessed with the mania of eating their own young. This disease (mania transitoria) arises from hyperemia of the brain.

Magnesium Phosphate is the earthy constituent of muscle and nerves. A disturbance of its molecular motion causes cramp and pains. As a nerve remedy it has furnished most excellent results. The nerve pains which are healed by **Magnesium phosphate** are generally of a shooting character, like lightning; boring,—often with the sensation of drawing [lacing] tightly together: they readily change their location, and are relieved by warmth and pressure.

Headache, face-ache, toothache, epigastric pains (pit of stomach), stomach-ache, and pains in the limbs of this description, I have frequently cured by this remedy. The pains of the stomach [bowels] generally radiate from the umbilicus, and are eased by pressure with the hand, by warmth, or by doubling up, and are sometimes accompanied by loose motions. In face-ache [neuralgic or rheumatic] which at its height is accompanied by an increased flow of tears, **Magnesium phosphate** is not suitable, but **Sodium chloride.**

The action of Magnesia is the reverse of that of Iron. By functional disturbance of the iron molecules, the muscular fibres relax; through the functional disturbance of the magnesium-molecules they contract. Therefore, **Magnesium phosphate** is the remedy for all cramps: spasms of the glottis, cramps of the legs, tetanus, lock-jaw, St. Vitus's dance, epilepsy, spasmodic ischury [stoppage of urine], etc.

Farmers give **Magnesium phosphate,** with very prompt results, for spasms and flatulent colic in horses, and for the acute [tympanitic] swellings of cattle, arising from unsuitable fodder. The inflammatory colic of horses requires *Ferric phosphate;* and if mortification commence, *Potassium phosphate.*

Potassium Phosphate is a constituent of the brain, the nerves, the muscles, and the blood-corpuscles. A disturbance in the function of the molecules of this salt causes

(A) In the brain—according to locality, extension, or intensity of disturbance,

(a) Mental depression, manifesting itself by irritability [vexation]; over-sensitiveness; tendency to weeping readily; timidity, shyness, terror.

(B) Softening of the brain,

(a) In the nerves, laming pains, mostly felt during rest; better from movement without exertion. Feeling of lassitude and exhaustion.

(b) In the muscle-cells, fatty metamorphosis. In the myosinc, or muscular juice, putrid decomposition.

(c) In the blood-corpuscles, too, rapid decay of the same.

Therefore, *Potassium phosphate* cures the following diseased conditions:—septic, scorbutic bleedings, mortification, encephaloid cancer, gangrenous croup, phagadenic chancre, putrid-smelling diarrhœa, adynamic, typhoid conditions, etc.

It will also be found useful in concussion of the brain, symptoms of collapse, and shocks of paralysis.

Calcium Phosphate is a constituent of the teeth, the bones, the connective-tissues, and the blood-corpuscles. It is-the specific remedy for rachitis (rickets), cranial tabes (wasting of the cranial bone), pallor, anæmia (bloodlessness), and chlorosis. It also assists teething and the callus formation of fractured bones, and is moreover the remedy for hydrocephalus.

It also cures those pains arising from anæmia, which are usually accompanied by a creeping sensation and a feeling of numbness or coldness.

Those cramps (epilepsy, etc.) which attack scrofulous persons are not always curable by *Magnesium Phosphate,* in which case *Calcium phosphate* is to be used.

Calcium phosphate is a restorative after acute disease.

Sodium Chloride is a constituent of all liquid and solid parts of the body. A disturbance in the motion of the molecules of this salt causes a change in the watery contents of such tissues; a change which exhibits itself in a decrease of secretions in the one case, or increase in the other[7].

Sodium chloride cures headache, toothache, face-ache (neuralgic or rheumatic); Pains of indigestion, if either flow of saliva or increased secretion of tears, vomiting of water or mucus accompany it; further, catarrhs of all the mucus membranes, with secretion of transparent, frothy, watery mucus; as also watery blisters, which burst and leave thin crusts.

The vomiting of, water, as well as the increased watery contents of the brain in acute diseases, such as typhus, scarlet fever, small-pox—showing itself in torpor (drowsiness); twitchings, jerkings of the limbs, etc.—are all caused by a functional disturbance of the molecules of this salt.

Potassium Chloride or muscle-salt stands in chemical relation to fibrin. A disturbance of molecular motion of this salt can produce a fibrinous exudation. *Potassium chloride,* therefore, corresponds to croupous and diphtheritic exudations. It cures Dysentery, summer Diarrhœa, Diphtheria, membranous Croup, croupous Inflammation of the lungs, fibrinous exudation in the interstitial connective-tissues (*i.e.* Mastitis), acute infiltration of the lymphatic glands, infiltrated inflammation of the skin, with or without vesicles (*i.e.* blistering Erysipelas), etc. *Potassium chloride* is the surest remedy for many diseases, especially of Eczema, which has been developed after vaccination with bad vaccine matter.

Calcium Fluoride is to be found in the surface of the bones and in the enamel of the teeth. On the grounds of therapeutical experiences, I assume that it is also a constituent of the elastic fibres, and that the proper function of these is promoted by this salt.

Elastic fibres are found in the epidermis (skin), in the connective-tissue, and in vascular walls.

A disturbance of the equilibrium of the molecules of Calcium fluoride causes a continued or chronically relaxed condition of the implicated fibres. If the elastic fibres of any portion of the vessels of the connective-tissue or of the lymphatic system have arrived at such a condition of relaxation, the absorption of a solid exu-

7 Example: *Increased* secretions of the mucus lining of the , digestive organ, with co-existing *decrease* of secretions of the mucus lining of the intestines ; consequently, indigestion, pains, and vomiting of mucus, with co-existing constipation.

dation in such a part cannot take place. In consequence, induration (hardening) of the part sets in. When the elastic fibres of the blood-vessels suffer a disturbance of the molecules of Calcium fluoride, such pathological enlargements of blood-vessels take place, which make their appearances as: hæmorrhoidal tumours, varicose (dilated) veins, and vascular tumours.

Silica is a component part of the connective-tissue, the epidermis, the hair, and the nails.

The effect attributed to it upon brain, spinal marrow, and nerves, must be referred to the connective-tissue covering of the nerve fibres.

A functional disturbance of Silica molecules causes a swelling of the affected portion of connective-tissue cells. This swelling may-remain stationery for some time, and then end in resolution, or suppuration.

Whitlow, furuncles, suppurations of glands and joints, deep-seated suppurations of cornea, etc., all fall within the sphere of Silica.

Silica cures also suppurations which have their origin in the Periosteum or connective-tissue membrane covering the bones.

Sodium Phosphate.

Through the presence of *Sodium phosphate,* lactic acid is decomposed into carbonic acid and water. The *Sodium phosphate* fixes or absorbs the carbonic acid and carries it to the lungs. Therefore, it is the remedy of those diseases which arise from an excess of lactic acid (pertaining to milk). It is specially suited to the troubles of young children who have been fed! with too much sugar and milk, and suffer from acidity.

The symptoms which indicate the use of *Sodium phosphate* are: Acid risings—vomiting of sour fluids or curdled masses; greenish Diarrhœa;—pains in the bowels, cramp, fever, with symptoms of acidity; Conjunctivitis, when the discharge is yellow gold-coloured, and thick like cream.—A coating of the tongue which is moist and of a deep yellow gold colour; similar coating on the palate and tonsils, etc.

Sodium Phosphate promises to be *the* remedy for polyuria. Sugar turns into lactic acid, and it is resolved into carbonic acid and water by the presence of the above salt. The quantity of lactic acid present being reduced by *Sodium phosphate,* room is made for the formation of new lactic acid from the sugar. The quantity of sugar is, consequently, reduced to its normal proportion by the *Sodium phos-*

phate.

Sodium Sulphate.

The use of **Sodium sulphate** (Glaubersalt) is indicated in the following conditions of disease: Gastric bilious conditions—vomiting of bile; watery bilious Diarrhœa; bitter taste, in the mouth. Bilious fever; intermittent fever with retching and ejection of bile; œdematous inflammation of the skin; smooth erysipelas; humid skin eruptions; and so on.

Potassium Sulphate and Calcium Sulphate.

The indications for the use of these two cell-salts will be found in the following chapter: special Guide in diseases.

The question whether this or that disease is or is not dependent on the existence of fungi is of no importance in biochemic treatment. If the remedies in the following special Guide are used, the therapeutical aim, that of curing disease, will be gained in the shortest way.

Long-standing chronic diseases, which have been brought on by overdosing, excessive use of medicines, as: Quinine, mercury, etc., can be cured by minute doses of cell-salts.

The symptoms decide the remedy.

But although the above-named diseases, caused by the abuse of medicines, can be cured: by taking cell-salts, it is self-evident that acute cases of poisoning by arsenic, phosphorus, etc., must be treated according to the well known principles relating to such conditions.

The inorganic substances present in the blood and tissues are sufficient to heal all diseases-which are curable at all.

SPECIAL GUIDE:

WHEN AND HOW TO USE THE INORGANIC TISSUE-FORMERS.

Generally, I make use of the sixth centesimal trituration, of which I give a dose every two hours in acute diseases; in chronic cases two or three times daily, a dose the size of a pea. In external injuries I apply the remedies also externally, in the proportion of a quantity as large as a pea, in a glass of water.

All Febrile and Inflammatory Conditions.

Ferric phosphate must be given in all diseases, when accompanied by heat and fever, in alternation with such special medicine as the other symptoms of the disease may require.

Group.

First give *Ferric phosphate* in alternation with *Potassium chloride* If these two remedies do not suffice, give *Calcium phosphate* and *Calcium fluoride,* also time about.

Inflammation of the Lungs.

Ferric phosphate and *Potassium chloride* are sufficient to cover most cases.

When a moist râle or wheezing of loose frothy rattling phlegm is heard, and the patient is almost unable to cough up the great quantity of mucus, *Potassium sulphate* or *Sodium chloride* are required. The nature and colour of the expectoration will decide the choice.

Bronchitis.

In Bronchitis or inflammation of the bronchial tubes or windpipe (chronic or acute), the same remedies apply, as in inflammation of the lungs.

Peritonitis, Pleurisy, Meningitis, and Pericarditis.

The more abundant the perspiration which follows *Ferric phosphate* given during the first stage of these diseases, the more rapidly *Potassium chloride,* given as the second remedy, will put an end to the process of disease.

Empyema—*Calcium sulphate* will be required.

Acute Articular Rheumatism. Rheumatic Fever.

Ferric phosphate suits the commencement of the disease, and suffices in most cases, followed by *Potassium chloride.*

After *Potassium chloride, Sodium chloride* and *Potassium sulphate* fit in. The latter especially corresponds with the wandering rheumatic pains of the joints. If some remnant of the disease still lingers after the above medication, give *Calcium phosphate*

Bright's Disease of the Kidney and Diabetes.

Sodium chloride and *Calcium phosphate* are the principal remedies.

According to the accompanying symptoms, other functional remedies may also have to be considered.

Puerperal (Child-bed) Fever.

In this disease *Potassium chloride* has to be given as chief remedy, then *Potassium phosphate.*

Typhoid, or Enteric Fever.

In typhoid the following remedies have to be considered: *Ferric phosphate Potassium chloride, Sodium chloride, Potassium phosphate,* and *Calcium phosphate*

Compare "Typhoid, adynamic symptoms."

Typhoid, Adynamic Symptoms.

When during an acute disease, accompanied by fever, such as diphtheria, scarlatina, smallpox, and so on, sopor (drowsiness) set in, or there be parched tongue, twitchings, watery vomiting, etc., *Sodium chloride* will be required. If there be sordes, a brown dirty-looking deposit on the teeth, putrid-smelling stools, septic bleedings, *Potassium phosphate* must be given.

Diphtheria.

Ferric phosphate subdues the fever, *Potassium chloride,* the exudation, or deposit in the throat.

If the face becomes pale and puffy, dryness of tongue set in, vomiting of watery fluids, dribbling of saliva, watery Diarrhœa, drowsiness, stertorous breathing, etc., *Sodium chloride* must be given.

Potassium phosphate is indicated in decidedly foul gangrenous conditions.

Should the diphtheritic exudation spread to the trachea, *Calcium phosphate* should be given in alternation with *Calcium fluoride.*

Summer Diarrhœa and Dysentery.

Ferric phosphate and *Potassium chloride* suffice in most cases.

Should delirium, tympanitis supervene, the stools have a putrid odour, then *Potassium phosphate* suits; as, also, if there be no symptoms of decay, but pure blood is passed with the stools.

For crampy, abdominal pains, eased by warmth, pressure, and doubling up— *Magnesium phosphate.*

Scarlet Fever.

In mild cases *Ferric phosphate* and *Potassium chloride* are alone sufficient—

Malignant cases must be treated by reference to remarks under the headings "Diphtheria" and "Typhoid adynamic symptoms."

Post-scarlatinal Dropsy is readily cured, according to the symptoms, by *Sodium chloride, Sodium sulphate,* and *Calcium sulphate.*

Small-pox,

Potassium chloride is the principal remedy. If adynamic symptoms arise, and those indicating blood decomposition, *Potassium phosphate* must be given. Salivation, sopor, and confluence of pustules require *Sodium chloride.*

Violent fever and considerable hyperæmia of brain at the beginning of the case may require *Ferric phosphate.*

Measles.

Ferric phosphate at first;—later on, such remedies as may be indicated by the eye or cough symptoms.

Head and Face Aches [Neuralgic Rheumatic].

Stitches or pressure, or throbbing, aggravated by shaking the head, by stooping, or, in fact, by every movement—*Ferric phosphate.*

Pains, accompanied by flushing and heat of the face—*Ferric phosphate.*

Pains, with vomiting of bile—*Sodium sulphate.*

Pains, with vomiting of transparent phlegm, mucus, or water—*Sodium chloride.*

Pains, with vomiting of food—*Ferric phosphate.*

Pains, with vomiting, hawking of white mucus—*Potassium chloride.*

Pains, vivid, shooting, stitching—intermittent and changing about—*Magnesium phosphate.*

Pains, of pale, sensitive, irritable [excitable] persons—*Potassium phosphate.*

Pains, fits of, with ensuing exhaustion—*Potassium phosphate.*

Pains which are worse in a warm room, and in the evening; better in the open, cool air—*Potassium sulphate.*

Pains, accompanied by the appearance of small lumps, nodules the size of a pea, upon the scalp—*Silica.*

Pains, with frothy, clear mucus covering the tongue, and torpid bowels—*So-*

dium chloride.

Pains, periodic, daily, recurring, with an abundant flow of acrid tears—*Sodium chloride.*

Pains, with a creeping sensation, feeling of coldness or of numbness—*Calcium phosphate.*

Pains, tearing, boring, gnawing; worse at night and from changes of weather—*Calcium phosphate.*

Children's headaches, as a rule, are readily cured "with *Ferric phosphate.*

Comotio Cerebri.

Disturbance of Brain Functions.

The functional *depression* of the affected brain-cells requires *Potassium phosphate.*

Hydrocephalic conditions—*Calcium phosphate.*

Chronic hydrocephalus—*Calcium phosphate.*

Cephalatomata—*Calcium fluoride.*

Cranial tabes—*Calcium phosphate.*

Fontanelles remaining too long open—*Calcium phosphate.*

If, in any of these diseases, putrid-smelling stools are present, *Potassium phosphate* must be given,

Delirium Tremens.

Most cases are readily cured by *Sodium chloride* Should the latter not suffice, give *Potassium phosphate.*

Vertigo (Giddiness), if occasioned by pressure of blood, is cured by *Ferric phosphate*; nervous vertigo by *Potassium phosphate* The coating of the tongue must also be considered, if there is any gastric (stomach) disturbance.

Ears.

Inflammatory ear-ache requires *Ferric phosphate.*

Inflammatory swelling of the, external meatus—*Silica.*

Discharge of thin yellow fluid from the ear—*Potassium sulphate.*

Discharge of thick yellow matter—*Calcium sulphate* and *Silica.*

Deafness, caused by swelling and catarrh of the Eustachian tubes and external meatus—*Potassium chloride, Potassium sulphate, Sodium chloride,* and *Silica.*

Rushing noises in the ears, caused by pressure of blood—*Ferric phosphate.*

Nervous noises in the ear—*Potassium phosphate.*

Mumps—*Potassium chloride;* and with abundant saliva—*Sodium chloride.*

Should orchitis occur, *Sodium chloride* must be taken.

With involuntary flow of tears—*Sodium chloride.*

With abundant flow of saliva-*Sodium chloride.*

With swelling of the gums and salivation—*Potassium chloride.*

With pains which change about—*Magnesium phosphate.*

With pains in pale, delicate, irritable persons—*Potassium phosphate.*

With easily bleeding gums—*Potassium phosphate.*

With pains which are located in the root-periosteum of the jaw—*Silica.*

With tearing, boring pains at night, worse from warmth or cold—*Calcium phosphate.*

With pains which are aggravated in the warm room, and in the evening, but better in open, cool air—*Potassium sulphate.*

With pains, accompanied by flushed, heated cheeks—*Ferric phosphate.*

With pains, aggravated by warm, relieved by cold, fluids—*Ferric phosphate.*

With pains, very vivid, made easier by warmth —*Magnesium phosphate.*

With swelling of the cheek [face]—First, *Potassium chloride,* then *Calcium sulphate.*

With hard swelling of the jaw—*Calcium fluoride.*

Complaints of Children during Dentition.

If fever is present, *Ferric phosphate;* —cramps with fever, *Ferric phosphate;* cramps without fever, *Magnesium phosphate* and *Calcium phosphate;*—inflammation of the eye, *Ferric phosphate, Calcium phosphate;* dribbling [at mouth], *Sodium chloride;* —spasm of the glottis, *Magnesium phosphate;* spasmodic cough, *Magnesium phosphate;*—spasm of the bladder, *Magnesium phosphate;*—diarrhœa, see heading "Diarrhœa."

Eyes.

On the eyelids, specks of matter, *Potassium chloride;* on the eyelids, yellow crusts of matter, ***Potassium chloride, Potassium sulphate.***

On the cornea, a blister, ***Potassium chloride.***

Flat abscess, of cornea, proceeding from a blister, ***Potassium chloride.***

Deep ulcer of the cornea, ***Silica, Calcium sulphate.***

Spots on the cornea, ***Potassium chloride, Calcium phosphate and Calcium fluoride.*** (Also externally).

Secretion of yellow, greenish matter, ***Potassium chloride, Potassium sulphate.***

Yellow creamy secretions, ***Sodium phosphate.***

White, mucous secretions, ***Potassium chloride.***

Light, transparent, mucous secretion, with acrid, smarting tears, ***Sodium chloride.***

Yellow mucous matter, ***Potassium sulphate.***

Thick, yellow matter, ***Calcium sulphate, Silica.***

Great redness, with severe pain, without mucus or matter, ***Ferric phosphate.***

Pains in the eye, commencing daily at certain times, with flow of tears, ***Sodium chloride.***

Styes [hordeoli], small lumps and indurations on the eyelids, ***Silica.***

Spasms of the eyelids [cramps], ***Magnesium phosphate*** and ***Calcium phosphate.***

Spasmodic squinting, ***Magnesium phosphate.***

Diplopia, sparks and rainbow colours before the eye, seeing many colours, ***Magnesium phosphate.***

Weak sight, after diphtheria, ***Potassium phosphate.***

Weak sight, after suppression of perspiration of feet, ***Silica.***

Hypopion, ***Calcium sulphate.***

Retina exudation, ***Potassium chloride*** In the first stages of the inflammation of the retina, ***Ferric phosphate.***

Cavity of Mouth.

CATARRHAL INFLAMMATION of the MUCOUS MEMBRANE covering the soft palate, tonsils, and pharynx.

If there is dry redness [inflammatory] and violent pain, ***Ferric phosphate.***

If white exudation, ***Potassium chloride.***

If a creamy, golden-yellow exudation, ***Sodium phosphate.***

If transparent, frothy mucus, ***Sodium chloride.***

If tonsils are enlarged or swollen, ***Potassium chloride*** will suit best, if there is a white or grayish-white coating on the tonsils.

If matter forms and suppuration threatens, ***Calcium sulphate, or*** Silica.

In chronic tonsilitis the proper remedy is Potassium chloride, Calcium phosphate, Sodium chloride.

INFLAMMATION OF TONGUE.—If much swollen, and of a deep, dusky red, ***Ferric phosphate*** In most cases this will suffice. If not, ***Potassium chloride*** If suppuration threatens, ***Calcium sulphate.***—For indurations, ***Silica, Calcium fluoride.***

Canker and scurvy, gangrenous, ***Potassium phosphate.***

GUMS.—If the gum be pale, ***Calcium phosphate*** is specially indicated; if it has a bright red edge, ***Potassium phosphate*** is required. The latter medicine is also required with bleedings of the gum.

Coatings of the Tongue.

A white, not slimy, covering requires ***Potassium chloride*** Slimy coating, and small bubbles of saliva on the edges, ***Sodium chloride.***

Tongue, as if spread with liquid dark mustard, and offensive breath, ***Potassium phosphate.***

Tongue of dirty brownish green, with a bitter taste in the mouth, ***Sodium sulphate.***

Tongue covered at the back, as if with yellow golden cream and moist, ***Sodium phosphate.***

Tongue covered with yellow slime, ***Potassium sulphate.***

The coating of the tongue does not always wholly influence the choice of a remedy in all affections of the tissues. It has, however, to be taken into consideration in those cases where I have taken note of it in this volume.—If any one who is suffering from a chronic catarrh of the stomach, takes also another (acute) disease, the coating of the tongue will not always have that peculiar appearance which will indicate the remedy suited to the acute disease.

If any disease—particularly of a chronic nature—shows itself without decisive symptoms, then the coating of the tongue will, in most cases, guide in the choice of an appropriate remedy.

Aphthæ and Stomatitis, *Potassium chloride, Potassium phosphate,* and *Sodium chloride;* the latter when there is much dribbling of saliva.

Noma, *Potassium phosphate.*

Vomiting.

Vomiting of food, *Ferric phosphate.*

Vomiting of food and acid fluids, *Ferric phosphate.*

Vomiting of bile, *Sodium sulphate.*

Vomiting of stringy transparent mucus, *Sodium chloride.*

Vomiting of watery fluid, *Sodium chloride.*

Vomiting of blood, *Ferric phosphate, Potassium chloride,* and *Sodium phosphate.*

Hawking up of white mucus, *Potassium chloride.*

Vomiting of acid fluids or curdy masses, *Sodium phosphate.*

Jaundice.

If it originates in a duodenal catarrh, *Potassium chloride* will be useful, *Potassium chloride* and *Sodium chloride.*

The coating of the tongue must determine the choice of a remedy.—Jaundice from vexation, *Sodium sulphate.*

Pains in Stomach and Abdomen.

GASTRITIS. *Acute Inflammation of the Stomach,* with violent pains of the distended organ, vomiting, and fever, *Ferric phosphate.*

If a case has come too late under treatment, and there are symptoms of exhaustion, dryness of tongue, etc., *Potassium phosphate* will have to-be given.

ACUTE AND CHRONIC PAINS OF THE STOMACH, which grow worse on taking food, or by pressure at the pit of the stomach, and particularly if vomiting of food occurs, *Ferric phosphate.*

Spasmodic cramping of the stomach, with clean tongue, requires *Magnesium phosphate.*

Pains with a crampy (spasmodic) tight [drawling] lacing sensation, *Magnesium phosphate.*

Pains of the stomach, with accumulation of water in the mouth, *Sodium chloride* If this does not altogether suffice, there is generally present a coating of the tongue, which requires *Potassium sulphate.*

Pressure, and a sensation of fulness, with yellow slimy coating of the tongue, *Potassium sulphate.*

Gnawing pains in the stomach, with flatulence [short belching of wind], affording no relief, *Magnesium phosphate.*

Colics, which are relieved by doubling up the body [bending double], rubbing, and in which eructations or hot applications give relief, require *Magnesium phosphate.*

Colic, with pain about the umbilicus, obliging the patient to bend double, *Magnesium phosphate.*

Flatulent colic of little children, which causes them to draw up their legs, with or without Diarrhœa, *Magnesium phosphate.*

If there is acidity, *Sodium phosphate* must be given.

Pains of indigestion, accompanied by vomiting,—the nature of the ejected matter indicates the remedy.

Gastric affections, with predominating acidity, *Sodium phosphate.*

Ulcers, ulceration of stomach, *Sodium phosphate.*

Diarrhœa.

Diarrhœa, watery, with abdominal pains, *Magnesium phosphate* and *Ferric phosphate* If the pain ceases, then returns, and is eased by bending double, *Magnesium phosphate.*

Diarrhœa, watery, and without pain, *Potassium phosphate.*

Diarrhœa, bilious, *Sodium sulphate.*

Diarrhœa, yellow slimy, *Potassium sulphate.*

Diarrhœa, white slimy, *Potassium chloride.*

Diarrhœa, bloody and bloody-slimy, *Potassium chloride.*

Diarrhœa, mattery, bloody-mattery, **Calcium sulphate.**

Diarrhœa, transparent, glassy [glairy], slime, **Sodium chloride.**

Stools of undigested food, **Ferric phosphate.**

Diarrhœa, putrid-smelling, **Potassium, phosphate.**

Diarrhœa, caused by excessive acidity, **Sodium phosphate.**

Hæmorrhoids.

The principal remedy is **Calcium fluoride** (See p. 45). As, besides the local Hæmorrhoids, disturbances in the function of the liver, the digestive organs, etc., are, as a rule, present; and stand in casual connection with the former, attention must be paid to those disturbances if a radical cure of hæmorrhoids is to be ensured.

Calcium fluoride has, therefore, to be taken alternately with another remedy, the choice of which is determined by the other or primary symptom. The remedies which will have to be most frequently considered, are: **Sodium chloride, Sodium sulphate,** and **Potassium sulphate.**

Polyuria, Excessive Secretion of Urine.

For theoretical reasons I recommend **Sodium phosphate** (See p. 46).

Bronchial Catarrhs, and Colds in the Head.

Sodium chloride cures colds, with clear watery or starch-like sputa. If feverishness accompanies the cold, **Ferric phosphate** must be given in alternation with any of the remedies that are indicated by the peculiar nature of the secretions; hence **Potassium sulphate** or **Sodium sulphate** may come into requisition. The same remedies apply to the discharges of mucus from the nose (frontal cavity) in colds of the head. Compare with "Diseases of the Mucous Membrane." **Potassium chloride** for "stuffy" colds, with discharge of thick white mucus. **Calcium fluoride** in obstinate cases.

Ozœna requires **Potassium phosphate** internally, and also applications of the same on the mucous lining of the nose.

Hoarseness.

Simple hoarseness from cold, **Potassium chloride;** rarely **Potassium sulphate** is required.—If caused by over-exertion of the vocal organs (as by speakers, actors, singers), **Ferric phosphate** is most useful; if necessary, also **Potassium phosphate.**

Coughs.

Short, acute, spasmodic, very painful, requires *Ferric phosphate,* then *Potassium chloride;* the true spasmodic cough, *Magnesium phosphate.*

As to accompanying discharges of mucus, etc., see section on "Diseases of the Mucous Membrane."

Hooping-Cough.

In inflammatory catarrhal stage, *Ferric phosphate;* for the nervous, spasmodic affection, *Magnesium phosphate Ferric phosphate* must be taken when there is vomiting of food. According to the nature of the mucus there may have to be chosen *Potassium chloride, Sodium chloride, or Potassium sulphate.*

Special symptoms may necessitate the alternate use of a suitable remedy, e.g., *Potassium phosphate or Calcium phosphate.*

Acute Œdema of the Lungs.

With dyspnœa, spasmodic cough with frothy expectoration of serous masses, *Sodium chloride,* and lividity of face, *Potassium phosphate.*

Diseases of the Mucous Membrane.

The colour and the consistency of the secretion must decide the choice of the remedy.

If the secretion is tough and sticky, *Potassium chloride* and *Calcium fluoride* must be taken; if it is fluid or slimy, *Sodium chloride, Potassium sulphate,* or *Sodium sulphate* may have to be given. *Potassium chloride* and *Calcium fluoride* are suitable when the secretion is white or yellowish white; *Sodium sulphate* when the phlegm is greenish yellow; *Sodium chloride* if it be watery, thick, or transparent. *Potassium phosphate* must be used when there is a chronic offensive defluxion from the nose.

The choice of the remedies has to be made in accordance with the above distinctions in cases of coughs with expectoration, in gonorrhœa, leucorrhoea, or "whites."

Inflammation, and Catarrh of the Bladder.

In acute cases, first of all *Ferric phosphate,* then *Potassium chloride* Chronic cases require *Potassium chloride, Sodium chloride, Potassium sulphate, or* Sodium sulphate, *according to the symptoms.*

Retention of Urine.

When spasm, cramp, is the cause of the retention or suppression of urine, Magnesium phosphate *is the remedy.* Ferric phosphate *cures the suppression of urine, accompanied by heat, as in little children.*

Involuntary Micturition at Night.

The first remedy to be given is Potassium phosphate. *If, after using this remedy for some weeks, no cure is effected, the accompanying symptoms must be sought for, and another cell-salt chosen in accordance with those symptoms.*

Eczema. Diseases of the Skin.

The remedies recommended for diseases of the mucous membrane are also suited to the diseases of the skin, viz: Potassium chloride, Calcium fluoride, Sodium chloride, Potassium sulphate *and* Sodium sulphate. *Eczema, lichen, etc., are included.*

Eczema, which has arisen after vaccination with bad lymph, requires Potassium chloride.

Intertrigo of children, chafing, Potassium chloride, Sodium chloride, Sodium sulphate; *with excess of acidity,* Sodium phosphate *must be given.*

Nettle-rash requires Potassium sulphate *and* Sodium chloride.

ERYSIPELS "ROSE."—The œdematous puffy inflammation of the skin requires *Sodium sulphate;* infiltrated or blistering erysipelas is cured by *Potassium chloride.*

Severe symptoms of fever and inflammation may accompany erysipelatous affections, and thus require *Ferric phosphate. Potassium sulphate* assists the scaling off of the skin.

Herpes zoster (shingles) requires *Potassium chloride* and *Sodium chloride.*

PEMPHIGUS.—Common pemphigus (blisters of various sizes with yellow watery contents and tense surface) requires *Sodium sulphate* Malignant pemphigus (blisters with watery-bloody contents and withered, wrinkled surface) requires *Potassium phosphate.*

BURNS AND SCALDS, of the first and second degrees, require *Potassium chloride.* If suppurating, *Calcium sulphate.*

Chilblains, if fresh, *Potassium chloride.*

Chilblains, if suppurating, *Calcium sulphate.*

If, at the commencement of any inflammation of the skin, *Ferric phosphate* is given, the disease can be prevented, or blighted in the germ. If that stage has passed in which this remedy is indicated, *Potassium chloride* must be given. If pus forms, then *Calcium sulphate* or *Silica* If the pus is dirty-looking and ichorous, and heavy-smelling, *Potassium phosphate* must be given. Proud flesh requires *Potassium chloride* In the same manner inflammation of fingers (whitlow) is treated. If the bone is implicated, *Calcium fluoride* is most suitable.

The treatment of blind boils, and bloody furuncles, carbuncles, etc., is as above. Hard scorbutic infiltrations of subcutaneous tissues are cured by *Potassium chloride* Scorbutic bleedings require *Potassium phosphate* Ingrown toe-nail requires *Potassium chloride* and local mechanical treatment.

Lupus requires *Potassium chloride, Calcium phosphate.*

Epithelioma, *Potassium sulphate.*

Effects of the bite of insects, *Sodium chloride* (used externally).

Warts on the hands, *Potassium chloride:* Dissolve a quantity, as large as a pea, of the triturated powder, in a tablespoonful of water, and moisten the part with this Solution.

Mastitis, Inflammation of the Breast.

Potassium chloride is indicated before matter has formed; when formed, and during its discharge, *Calcium sulphate* and *Silica* are indicated.

Calcium fluoride is required when the edges round the suppurating part are hard or callous.

When the pus is offensive, unhealthy, of a brownish nature, *Potassium phosphate.*

Hard knots, or lumps in breast, require *Calcium fluoride* and *Silica.*

Lymphatic Glands.

For acute infiltration (swelling), *Potassium chloride* Chronic cases of swollen glands may require *Potassium chloride, Calcium phosphate, Calcium fluoride* If inclined to suppurate, and during suppuration, *Calcium sulphate* and *Silica* are required, and *Calcium fluoride* when the edges round the suppuration are callous.

Chancre and Gonorrhœa.

Chancre—the principal remedy is **Potassium chloride** (in the third trituration) internally and externally, used alternately with **Sodium chloride** Will cure uncomplicated cases speedily[8].

Phagadenic chancre requires **Potassium phosphate** Hard chancre, **Calcium fluoride** (internally and externally).

Chronic syphilis corresponds to **Potassium chloride, Sodium chloride, Sodium sulphate, Calcium fluoride,** and **Silica,** according to the symptoms.

Ferric phosphate cures the inflammatory stage of gonorrhœa; for further details see the chapter on "Diseases of the Mucous Membrane."

Besides the internal use of the remedy corresponding to the symptoms, it is advisable to bathe the parts twice daily in a solution of the same remedy.

Orchitis, after suppression of gonorrhœa, requires **Potassium chloride;** eventually **Potassium sulphate** and **Sodium chloride.**

Warts require **Potassium chloride; Calcium phosphate,** also, externally.

Hydrocele, **Sodium chloride, Calcium phosphate.**

Induration (hardening) of testicles, **Calcium fluoride, Silica.**

Scrotal œdema, **Sodium sulphate, Sodium chloride.**

Preputial œdema, **Sodium sulphate, Sodium chloride.**

Mechanical Injuries.

Cuts and other fresh wounds, bruises, and sprains, require **Ferric phosphate.**—If, after the use of this, any swelling of the contused parts remains, give **Potassium chloride** If suppuration sets in, in neglected cases, give **Calcium sulphate** and **Silica.** Ichor or mortification necessitate **Potassium phosphate;** proud flesh, **Potassium chloride.**

Fracture of bone requires (along with mechanical treatment) at first, for injuries of the soft parts, **Ferric phosphate;** then **Calcium phosphate,** to promote the formation of new bony matter to unite the fractured bone.

TENALGIA CREPITANS (crackling of the sinews), which occurs on the dorsal side of the lower arm above the wrist in the case of carpenters and other artisans,

8 The powder applied on the moistened part.

by pressing their chisel or other tool too hard in a rotatory motion against the material on which they were working, has been quickly cured in two cases by means of *Ferric phosphate.*

A third case, which had become chronic under ordinary treatment, I cured easily with *Potassium chloride,* after *Ferric phosphate* proved ineffectual.

Ulcers of the Lower Limbs.

Under this head any of the remedies given for diseases of the skin and mucous membrane, and *Silica* in addition, may have to be employed.

Calcium fluoride cures varicose ulceration.

Diseases of the Bone.

If the surrounding *soft parts* are red, inflamed, hot, and painful, *Ferric phosphate.* Against ulceration of bone, *Calcium fluoride, Silica,* and *Calcium phosphate.* Exudations: hard, rough, corrugated elevations on the bone surface require *Calcium fluoride* This remedy is even better than *Silica* in cases of Cephalhæmatomata (so-called blood-tumour) on the parietal bones of new-born children.

RICKETS, *Calcium phosphate.* If atrophy ensues, with foul diarrhœa, this condition must first be subdued by *Potassium phosphate* Should there be any excess of acidity, it must be removed by *Sodium phosphate.*

Hip-joint disease—*Ferric phosphate. Potassium chloride, Silica,* and *Calcium fluoride.*

Anæmia, Chlorosis (bloodlessness).

The remedy of true anœmia, chlorosis, is *Calcium phosphate* As soon as a decided improvement of general health sets in, *Ferric phosphate* may follow. *Potassium chloride* may have to be given as a secondary remedy, if such symptoms as Eczema, eruptions of the skin, exist, for which this remedy is beneficial.

Conditions resembling chlorosis require *Sodium chloride* and *Potassium phosphate,* the choice to be decided by the characteristic accompanying symptoms.

Potassium phosphate cures pallor or bloodless-ness, which has been caused by long-continued depression of the mind.

Hæmorrhage. Bleedings.

Blood, red, readily coagulating into a jellylike mass, *Ferric phosphate.*

Black, thick, tough blood requires *Potassium chloride.*

Pale-red or blackish-red, but thin and watery, not coagulating *Potassium phosphate* and *Sodium chloride.*

Epistaxis, bleeding from the nose (in children) is, as a rule, generally cured by *Ferric phosphate* Predisposition to nasal hæmorrhages, *Potassium phosphate.*

Uterine hæmorrhage, *Calcium fluoride.*

Hæmorrhoidal bleedings, *Ferric phosphate, Potassium chloride,* and *Calcium fluoride.*

Menstruation.

If occurring too early and too profusely, *Potassium chloride;* if too late and scanty, *Potassium sulphate; Potassium phosphate* in pale, sensitive persons, who weep easily. If menses are suppressed, *Potassium phosphate* and *Potassium chloride;* or, in accordance with the attending symptoms, another remedy may be selected. If leucorrhoea accompanies the suppression, or if menstruation is too profuse or too scanty, then the peculiarity of the leucorrhoea must indicate the remedy. A mild white leucorrhoea indicates *Potassium chloride;* a mild yellow, *Potassium sulphate;* an acrid, corroding discharge, "whites," *Sodium chloride.*

Labour Pains.

Irregular, weak pains require *Potassium phosphate.*

Spasmodic, crampy pains, *Magnesium phosphate.*

Menstrual Colic.

Magnesium phosphate suits this colic generally. *Potassium phosphate* suits sensitive, irritable, pale, or lachrymose persons.

With accelerated pulse, increased redness of face, etc., *Ferric phosphate* is to be given.

VAGINISMUS, *Ferric phosphate, Magnesium phosphate.*

Pains in the Nape of the Neck, the Back and Limbs. Neuralgic, Rheumatic,

Pains only felt during motion, or made worse by motion, *Ferric phosphate;* second remedy, *Potassium chloride.*

Pains which are laming, but improved by moderate exercise, are increased by exertion (walking too much), and especially worse after rising from a sitting position (at the commencement of motion), require *Potassium phosphate.*

Pains, with a feeling of numbness, or creeping, or a sensation of coldness, worse at night and during rest, require *Calcium phosphate.*

Pains, vivid, shooting, boring, intermittent, shifting, neuralgic, require *Magnesium phosphate.*

Pains, rheumatic-gouty, *Potassium chloride, Sodium chloride, Calcium phosphate.*

Pains which are worse in warm rooms, and in the evening; better in open cool air, *Potassium sulphate.*

Pains which the patient cannot describe very clearly, accompanying symptoms must decide the remedy, such as an eruption, coating of the tongue, etc.

Chronic articular rheumatism requires *Potassium chloride, Sodium chloride, Calcium phosphate, Potassium sulphate.*

For the cracking of joints in chronic articular rheumatism Dr. Kafka recommends *Sodium chloride.*

Lumbago, *Ferric phosphate, Calcium phosphate.*

Sciatica, *Potassium phosphate, Magnesium phosphate.*

Chronic scrofulous swelling of the knee requires *Sodium chloride, Calcium phosphate,* and *Calcium fluoride.*

For suppurations of the joints, *Calcium sulphate* and *Silica.*

Hygroma patellæ, "Housemaid's knee," requires *Sodium chloride* and *Calcium phosphate.*

Cramps and other Nervous Affections.

Nervous palpitation requires *Potassium phosphate* (Palpitation caused by pressure of blood requires *Ferric phosphate* and *Potassium chloride.*)

Asthma requires *Potassium phosphate* and *Potassium chloride* Asthma with excess of frothy mucus requires *Sodium chloride.*

Spasms of the glottis, tetanus, lockjaw, cramp in the legs, St. Vitus's dance, etc., are cured by *Magnesium phosphate.*

In Epilepsy the following remedies have to be considered:—

Ferric phosphate, in rush of blood to the head. *Potassium phosphate,* if, during a fit, the face is very pale and sunken; body and limbs cold, and if there is much palpitation after the fit.

Silica, nocturnal fits of epilepsy—occurring especially at changes of the moon.

Magnesium phosphate and Calcium phosphate, if the above-named symptoms are not present.—*Calcium phosphate* is particularly suitable for young persons whose bodies are in the stage of development, and also in scrofulous cases.

Other co-existing disease symptoms occurring in the intervals have to be considered in the choice of a remedy. *Potassium chloride* is indicated if the epileptic patient has or has had eczema.

Paralysis or lameness, caused by exhaustion of nerve power, requires *Potassium phosphate* (only recent cases are curable).

Cases of recent rheumatic lameness require *Ferric phosphate.*

Rheumatic lameness, *Potassium chloride, Calcium phosphate.*

Silica is indicated where suppressed perspiration of the feet is found to have been the cause.

Gouty deposit requires *Silica* and *Calcium fluoride.*

Ague—Intermittent Fever.

The specific remedy is indicated by any one of the co-existing symptoms below-named:

Vomiting of food, *Ferric phosphate.*

Vomiting of bile, *Sodium sulphate.*

Vomiting of water or mucus, *Sodium chloride.*

White coating of tongue, *Potassium chloride.*

Yellow slimy coating of tongue, *Potassium sulphate.*

Tongue moist, clear mucus covering the tip, but clean at the back, requires *Sodium chloride.*

Perspiration, abundant, exhausting, heavy-smelling, *Potassium phosphate.*

Perspiration, decidedly acid, *Sodium phosphate.*

Sour taste in the mouth, vomiting of sour masses, *Sodium phosphate.*

Tendency to bleeding of the gums, *Potassium phosphate* See "Gums, bright red edge."

In the case of delicate, pale, nervous patients, ague requires ***Potassium phosphate,*** if no very special symptoms (see above) indicate another remedy.

Ague-patients must abstain from milk diets, butter-milk, eggs, fat, or fish.

He who diagnoses very exactly will readily and comparatively speedily cure ague or intermittent fever by the use of the above-mentioned tissue-salts.

Dropsy.

Caused by loss of blood or vital fluids, ***Calcium phosphate*** and ***Ferric phosphate.***

Post-scarlatinal dropsy can be cured by ***Sodium chloride, Sodium sulphate,*** and ***Calcium sulphate.***

Simple dropsy of the areolar tissue has to be treated with ***Sodium sulphate*** and ***Sodium chloride.***

Dropsy occasioned by cardiac disease, liver or kidney disease, the remedy has to be selected according to the prominence of the accompanying symptoms.

[The following Clinical Cases have been collected from various Medical Journals, and from the practice of qualified Medical Practitioners.

It will be seen that most of the cases which Dr. Schüssler has put on record here have been treated by other medical men. These give conclusive proof of the merits of the Bio-chemic treatment of disease.]

CLINICAL CASES.

APRIL, 1879. M. K., aet. 16, has suffered for years from periodically returning headaches. The pain is concentrated in the right temple, and of a boring nature, as if a screw were being driven in—as the patient expresses herself. Preceding this pain there is a burning sensation at the pit of the stomach, bitter taste in the mouth, and lassitude. These symptoms are only felt at night, or in the morning. When the attack comes on, the patient is quite unable to attend to any ordinary duties. Generally vomiting of bile follows, and then improvement sets in. ***Sodium sulphate*** daily; as much as a bean, dissolved in water, and taken repeatedly, cured the young lady entirely.

M. L., a gentleman aet. 38, took a chill while in a state of perspiration. He suffered in consequence from tearing pains in the limbs, noises in the ears, with dulness of hearing and frontal headache. These pains were accompanied by fever, and although he had night-sweats they brought no relief. The appetite was poor, and the tongue covered with a white coating. I gave a small quantity of *Potassium chloride* in water, every two hours. A rapid general improvement set in, but pains and numbness in the feet were still present. Also the habitual perspiration of feet was still absent. At this stage the patient received *Silica*—2 doses daily for a week. Perspiration of feet was re-established, and on the re-appearance of this, the rest of the ailments left him, and health was quite restored.

MAY, 1879. J. D., a man of 69 years of age, had been complaining for several weeks of pains in the limbs, which settled in the right leg, from the hip down to the ankle, but were worst at the joints, being of a shifting nature—intermittent—sometimes shooting and darting like lightning, causing the patient to change his position frequently. Warmth gives him relief. He is unable to leave his bed: is almost in despair, thinking he is dying. *Magnesium phosphate;* a dose every three hours. The improvement on taking this remedy was marked and rapid. But whenever he stopped with the medicine, he felt worse again. By continuing steadily with *Magnesium phosphate,* a complete cure was effected.

I was called to attend a girl 12 years of age. She had had some time ago, an attack of rheumatic fever. I found the little patient, who had been taken ill the previous day, in bed. The joints of both knees were swollen, somewhat red, and very painful. The joints of the vertebræ at the nape of the neck were implicated, and every movement out of the constraint position of the neck and back was very painful. Her friends expected that salicylic acid would be applied, which they had already seen used, but I gave *Ferric phosphate* and *Potassium chloride* alternately every three hours. Next day, to the astonishment of the friends, the fever and pains were less, and the knees were quite free from pain. Now I ordered *Potassium chloride* to be given alone for the swelling, and the next morning on my return I found all the symptoms worse. I repeated the *Ferric phosphate* again, and there was a rapid improvement. But in the same degree as the pains were leaving and the swelling decreasing, spasmodic pains in the abdomen set in. There was also an occasional vomiting of bilious matter. As soon as these latter symptoms came on, I ordered the little patient some *Magnesium phosphate* dissolved in water, in frequent sips, which removed all these symptoms in 24 hours. *Ferric phosphate* and *Potassium chloride* were continued in less frequent doses. Six days after my first visit the patient was able to leave the bed, and was quite well.

DR. SCHLEGEL

NOTES BY THE EDITOR OF THE "MONTHLY MEDICAL JOURNAL."

From this clinical report it is very evident that the proper application of Dr. Schüssler's method has surprisingly favourable results. We have repeatedly occasion to recommend these medicines, as they are so reliable in rheumatic fever (acute articular rheumatism).

DECEMBER, 1879. A little girl, aged nine, had recovered from Diphtheria and Scarlatina rather easily, and was allowed to be in the convalescent room. Suddenly she began to-swell without any apparent cause. Her face became puffy; the feet also œdematous to above the ankles. Urine scarcely decreased; containing no albumen. No pain over the kidneys on pressure. Pulse somewhat feverish; but appetite, sleep, and stools still natural. I gave three different medicines—amongst these, Aconitum—without success. Dropsy (amasarca et ascites) are increasing rapidly; urine scanty; only very small quantities occasionally, being slightly turpid, and containing much albumen. Whether any epithelical sheathings were present was not ascertained. Kidneys were now more sensitive to pressure. Consciousness always present. *Sodium chloride* alone cured this case in about a. fortnight.

DR. COHN.

FROM THE "CLINICAL TIMES."

In August, 1877, a young man who had suffered from sciatica some years ago, and had been in the habit of having subcutaneous injections of morphia, developed a boil on the seat. This discharged freely, and would not heal. When at last it seemed to be healed and was comparatively well, the patient took cold. While at a military review he was caught in a heavy rain. Suppuration began again, and this time the discharge was excessive. His mother became alarmed, as he was very weak and had no appetite. His sleep was disturbed, and he felt a constant thirst I prescribed *Silica*—a dose every morning on an empty stomach. After one week the mother was able to furnish the very favourable report:—"The discharge of matter has been reduced so much that at one time it seemed gone altogether. The great thirst has left him, and his appetite has returned; his sleep is sound, and the shivery, chilly feeling he had has completely gone." **Silica** has here furnished a brilliant demonstration of its power over suppuration, with its characteristic accompanying symptoms.

DR. GOULLON, JR.

Dr. F., of Alsò, Hungary, reports:—I was requested to go into the country to see a man who had been suffering the last three days from spasmodic convulsive sobbing. He was lying in bed. Subcutaneous injections of morphia, friction with chloroform and sinapisms (mustard poultices) were all of no use. Although the sobbing was mitigated for two or three hours, it returned with more violence than ever. I gave him a powder of **Magnesium phosphate** in half a tumblerful of water. After the second tablespoonful the sobbing ceased altogether, to the astonishment of all those present.

I had fifteen cases of rheumatic fever. They were all successfully and rapidly cured with **Ferric phosphate.**

A hard swelling under the chin about the size of a pigeon's egg disappeared completely in about four weeks under the use of **Calcium fluoride.** Both old and new school medicines had failed to cure.

In Diphtheria (maligna), where every known remedy failed, **Potassium phosphate** with, or sometimes without, **Sodium chloride** effected subsidence of malignity, and hastened the cure,

In Paralysis after Diphtheria, I know of no better remedy than **Potassium phosphate.**

A very interesting case came under my treatment, which deserves the attention of the profession. I was called to a lady advanced in years. She had been suffering for nearly five weeks from fearful attacks of convulsive spasms. During the last twenty-four hours she had had 30 attacks. The spasms darted through her body like an electric shock, so that she fell to the ground. The attack lasted a few minutes, after which she felt well enough, but rather exhausted. The sufferer did not venture to leave her bed now, afraid of further injuries. She had been treated by her first doctor with Flor. Zinci., Fowler's Solution, and cold friction, but without success.

When I saw the lady I thought of trying Schüssler's functional remedies. Knowing that ***Magnesium phosphate, Potassium phosphate,*** and ***Calcium phosphate*** are prescribed for allaying spasms (cramp), I chose the latter, ***Calcium phosphate,*** under these circumstances. Next day, to the astonishment of those' about her, I found the old lady walking about the room. She met me with a smile, exclaiming—"Ah, Doctor, my spasms are cured." And so it was. She had not had another attack.

DB. FECHTMANN.

Reuter, a master shoemaker of Berlin, aet. 40, was taken fill, after catching cold, as he stated. There was fever and violent pain in the right shoulder. The first visit I paid was on the third day after he had been taken ill, Nov. 21st Temperature high, pulse full and quick, thirst and loss of appetite. The right shoulder was very red, and sensitive to the touch. He was not able to lie in his bed, as the pressure of the pillows was unbearable. He was lying on the sofa supported with cushions, so that the shoulder should be free. from pressure. I gave my patient ***Ferric phosphate,*** as much as would cover a sixpenny piece. This was dissolved in a large glassful of water, and a teaspoonful of the solution given every hour. Improvement was felt oven after a few hours. During the night the patient was able to sleep, and on the following day the. fever abated. On the 25th Nov. the patient was able to move the arm pretty freely. Nov. the 28th he tried to work; but feeling the weight of his hammer too much, he rested a few days longer, when he felt himself quite well.

DR. K SULZER.

MARCH 2ND. Dr. Fisher was consulted by a lady (***enciente***) who was suffering from a cough which caused great inconvenience, as with every cough there was emission of; urine. ***Ferric phosphate*** cured her very speedily. A short time ago the lady under similar circumstances was again troubled with a cough. ***Ferric phosphate*** this time also cured her as speedily.

Dr. Köck, of Munich, reports:—In thirty-five cases of measles which came under my treatment, coryza and bronchial catarrh were very slight in the premonitory stage. Conjunctivitis and intolerance of light along with it were the more prominent symptoms. Within a few days after, the rash appeared, lasting five or six days, and then disappeared. But either during the blush of the rash or the fading of it, painful swelling of one or both glands below the ear set in. The children again became feverish, and were crying and moaning both day and night. The remedy which I choose was ***Ferric phosphate;*** and according to the violence of the fever, I ordered a spoonful of the solution every hour or two. I gave it at the premonitory stage, and when I saw that it proved very satisfactory, I looked for no other remedy. For the glandular swelling, external redness and painfulness, I used the same medicine, and my cases ended very satisfactorily.

In September last autumn I was in the Highlands. The dairymaid of a farmer there spoke to me, saying she had hurt her thumb while sharpening a scythe. The case proved to be this:—The whole thumb of the left hand was swollen, and of a bluish-red colour, and very painful when touched, much inflamed, and there was a small wound at the extensor side at the joint above the nail. On pressure there was a whitish-yellow discharge mixed with white shreds. Both phalanges were easily displaced, and a peculiar noise was-heard, which I had observed before in similar cases. This fact made me decide on giving ***Calcium fluoride*** The medical man in the village whom the farmer had consulted said amputation was the only thing that could be done for the case. She took ***Calcium fluoride,*** and some time after the farmer had occasion to see me, when he informed me that the servant's thumb was quite well.

A woman, aged 56, from Simbach, who always wore blue spectacles, came to see me, as she had become blind in the right eye. The cause and consequent suffering were as follows:—Three years ago, on the 15th Jan., at twelve o'clock noon, she was walking from Arnstorf to Simbach. The whole of the meadows were covered with snow, on which the sun was shining brightly, causing a strong refraction. Suddenly she felt a severe pain in the right eye, and immediately discovered that she had lost the sight of it She took some snow and held it over her eye, which, she thought did her some good. On reaching home she sent for the Doctor, who put a leech to the right temple and gave her a strong purgative. She had to keep her bed for three weeks. The pain subsided, but her sight did not return. Some time after, she travelled all the way to Passau to consult Dr. E., the oculist. He gave a laxative and some ointment to be rubbed all around the eye (***Ungunt: Hydrarg:***). As the ointment affected the gum and loosened her teeth, she stopped using it, her sight being no better. Later on, when she heard that Professor Rothmund had operated on the pastor of Landau for cataract, she went to see him. "If this medicine won't help you, you will remain blind for life," were the Professor's words. His prescription was Kali

Iodide. After having had the prescription made up three times, and using it steadily, she felt no improvement, and was quite inconsolable. With her right eye she saw nothing—all seemed smoke and mist; and the other eye was becoming weaker and weaker from month to month. External examination showed the conjunctiva intact, as also the cornea, iris, &c. All pointed to internal disease of the inner medium of the eye. I could see but little of the retina, as there was a kind of mist over it, which seemed to spread from the vitrous humour over the background of the eye. I introduced the rays of light in different directions, and by this means I was better able to obtain sight of the retina. It appeared dim and misty, the veins were clearly seen forming a dark network. In some places there were indistinctly defined spots, some larger than others, appearing to me like the residue of extravasated blood. The arteries were scarcely visible, and seemed to me pale and more contracted than in the normal condition. The necessary therapeutic treatment clearly indicated to me was to produce absorption of the exuded substance, this being the cause of the dulness of sight According to Professor Rothmund's opinion, inflammation of the retina always arises in the connective-tissue, and as this exuded substance appears of a coagulating nature, which no doubt is fibrinous, and, as is well known, can be hypertrophied, and is capable of fatty degeneration, I found that of the remedies I could think of, the most suitable seemed to be ***Potassium chloride*** I now gave the woman eight powders, each containing two centigrams; the powder to be dissolved in half a wineglassful of water, a tablespoonful to-be taken night and morning. A fortnight after, the patient came back, saying—"I don't think I am any worse; please-to give me some more of these powders." She received a dozen, with the same directions. One morning she called quite early, and told me in great glee that on rising that morning she could see the window-sash quite distinctly. I tested her sight from different distances, and found that she-had really improved. "I can see pretty well through the mist," she said. ***Potassium chloride*** was continued in small doses, and in four months her sight was restored.

JUNE 16TH. Dr. Köck writes:—An old woman came to me, 72 years of age. She had worn a green shade over her eyes to my own recollection since my younger days, when as a student I spent my holidays at Simbach with my grandparents. This person complained of a constant burning sensation in her eyes, causing a continued flow of smarting tears. This commenced at eight o'clock in the morning and lasted till sunset During the night it was better. She bad much thirst, but little appetite. Externally the conjunctiva palpebrarum was in a chronic state of inflammation. On either side of the nose there was excoriation and eczema of the skin, caused by the flow of acrid tears. The punctæ lachrymosa were dilated; but the tear ducts were unobstructed. I hesitated whether I should give **Sodium chloride** or **Arsenic;** but Dr. Schüssler's special mention of" **Sodium chloride** in regard to these excessive lachrymose secretions determined my choice, and I gave **Sodium chloride** in water; one teaspoonful three times a day. In three weeks the symptoms all greatly subsided, and shortly after entirely disappeared.

AUGUST 17TH. Dr. Köck informed us a farm servant came to him, and be said be could not see. Some time before this a piece of wood bad struck him in the eye. He bad been treated for it; had had purgatives, leeches, and cold water applications, and now his sight was quite gone. The particulars of the case were these. The bulbus was infiltrated with vascular engorgement. The conjunctiva was swollen, rand the eyelid also in an irritated and inflamed condition. The cornea was dim, with a smoky appearance of the anterior chamber (*i.e.,* between the cornea and iris), and some matter could be seen floating quite distinctly. I found no foreign body. The subjective results were—severe burning pain in the eye as if from a foreign body, and continuous flow of tears. The man had to keep his eye tied up. His appetite was good, and pulse normal As to the therapeutic treatment, I had evidently to deal with two different affections—Hypopion (matter in the eye) and conjunctivitis.

First of all, I gave **Ferric phosphate,** a dose every two hours, and in a week the burning pain and watering of the eye were less. One week after this the man complained that his sight had not improved. Now, I had the task of absorption of the matter before me, as well as the clearing of the cornea. To meet the first condition I gave Hep. sul.; but after a fortnight I could recognise no special progress. I felt rather in a fix with the case, as absorption would not take place. Remembering an expression of Dr. Quagleo, at M., that he considered **Calcium** a still more powerful medicine, I gave some **Calcium sulphate,** to be taken in water in three doses. Scarcely a week after, the man came to me greatly delighted, saying that he could see gleams of light in the right eye. Positively, I found the cornea less cloudy, and could observe that some of the matter had been absorbed. Whenever I find improvement certain I decrease the dose. I now gave him only a dose night and morning. In three weeks absorption was complete, and dimness of the cornea quite removed, and his sight restored. Besides this all the inflammation of the conjunctiva was also cured.

AUGUST, 1880. A swelling under the chin the size of a pigeon's egg was considerably reduced by *Potassium chloride;* but still there was induration (hardness) and an uneven surface. *Calcium fluoride* taken for a few days caused it to disappear altogether. Shortly after its disappearance the patient had slight conjunctivitis with swelling, which *Potassium chloride* soon cured.

Dr. K.

AT A MEETING OF MEDICAL MEN AT SCHAFFHAUSEN, Professor Dr. Rapp said;—"In my opinion the greatest merits of Dr. Schüssler's method lie in the introduction of *Potassium phosphate* and *Magnesium phosphate* In ordinary stomatitis, with swelling of the gums, deposit on the teeth and foul breath, *Potassium phosphate* has given very satisfactory proofs of its value."

In Asthma, when the patient's attacks come on after taking food, and his colour becomes bad, or when there is rapid emaciation or sunken eyes, Dr. Rapp recommends the *Potassium* remedies.

DECEMBER, 1879. Dr. Crüwell reports on incontinence of urine:—When I became acquainted with Dr. Schüssler's preparations, I was very anxious to test the effects of *Potassium phosphate,* as Dr. Schüssler recommends this against paralysis and paralytic conditions. Whoever has been occupied with the study of psychology is naturally ready to suspect paralysis everywhere. I acknowledge I may have given *Potassium phosphate* too frequently, as I was desirous to find out what it could do. For various reasons it led me to give it for incontinency. I gave it three to four times daily in a little water. In five cases, two of which I treated without good results, *Potassium phosphate* brought about amazingly rapid improvement. With a young girl of seven I had until lately to repeat the remedy every time it was given up, as the incontinency always returned when it was discontinued. The most successful case was that of an old gentleman of sixty. No doubt in this case there was a sub-paralytic condition of the sphincter muscle. Some months after treatment he called back to say he was perfectly cured, but desired to have some of the powders, simply by way of precaution.

A lady, 29 years of age, of sanguine temperament, and rather high colour of face, has been suffering the last five years from the following indigestion troubles, which she contracted by a draught of very cold water whilst in a state of heat and perspiration. She has no desire to eat; great dislike to milk. After food, nausea and vomiting of food, which is so acid that it sets her teeth on edge. She can take nothing sour. Meat, and also salt herring, cause much pain, and so do cake and coffee. The sickness and retching occasionally come on before breakfast; otherwise only after food. To this is added Cephalalgia. She feels a beating pain in her forehead and temples; formerly on the left, now more on the right side. This pain is most violent. Catamenia appears every three weeks, with much loss; dragging pain in lower abdomen and lumbar region. The motions are normal, the sleep is disturbed by anxious dreams, and feels in the morning as though she had been beaten. In the evening she feels oppressed and swelled, so that she has to loosen her dress; she cannot wear it in the least tight. Her pulse is accelerated 100 per minute. As a girl she was quite healthy, and had never suffered from anæmia On the whole, the lady was not much emaciated, in spite of her ailing so long. This was the description the patient gave of her case. The leading symptoms of this case led me to choose iron. I ordered her a dose of Dr. Schüssler's saccharated trituration, to be taken before meals, about the size of a bean, 3 times daily. When I saw her again she was able to give me the very satisfactory report, that her ailments were cured.

DR. MOSSA.

MARCH, 1880. Dr. Mossa, Bamberg, reports:—Towards the end of last year I received a letter with the following details, and asking me to forward some medicine:—"My boy, a child of seven, hitherto healthy and strong, has been suffering from pains in the stomach for some weeks. The pains commenced about the umbilicus, and extended to the pit of the stomach. Latterly he has vomited all his food, sometimes immediately after taking it, and at other times not till during the night. The child has now become very emaciated. Last week he had an attack of intermittent fever. It has, however, not returned since taking the medicine our doctor here has given him. The boy complains of much exhaustion." To form a scientific diagnosis of the case on such information was clearly impossible; but, as it was not convenient for me personally to examine the case, I had to do my best with the details furnished. The nature of the abdominal pains pointed to swelling and enlargement of the organs of the viscera—liver, spleen, &c.; also the attack of intermittent fever, probably subdued by quinine, and the vomiting of food all coincided with my surmises. As to the selection of the medicine I hesitated considerably, and then decided to give *Ferric phosphate;* twelve powders; one night and morning. The report some time after was very favourable. The fever had not returned; the vomiting of food and pains in the stomach had quite ceased soon after taking the medicine. The little fellow was feeling so much stronger that he attended school again.

Dr. Goullon, jun., who used *Potassium chloride* with much success in a swelling of the feet and lower extremities, adds the following particular indications for its use. The remedy in question appears indicated in chronic persistent swelling if the feet and lower limbs, when the swelling is soft at first, afterwards becoming hard to the touch, without pain or redness. It is, however, itchy; and at one stage may be termed snowy white and shining. Lastly, the swelling becomes less perceptible in the morning than in the evening; but may acquire such dimensions as to cause great tension, with a feeling as if it would burst.

A case from a contributor may here be mentioned, which was cured by *Potassium chloride:*—A lady, Mrs. B., suffering from swelling of the leg below the knee, had been seen some months by her doctor, who had poulticed it, and had opened it with the lancet; but there was no discharge. She was unable to walk. It was then painted with Iodine without effect; then bandaged to reduce the excessive hard swelling, and cold water poured over it thrice a day. Some parts were blue-looking on removing the bandage. It felt cold and very hard, and looked as if ready to burst; almost twice its usual size. Warm fomentations and *Potassium chloride* taken internally and applied externally, cured the leg in three weeks.

JULY 29, 1879. From the reports of a medical congress At Dortmund, by Dr. Stens, junior:—

I should like to report on a case of rheumatism, which 'was cured by *Ferric phosphate* in a very short time, after having tried several of the most reputed remedies which seemed indicated. A lady of about forty-two years of age (catamenia normal, though scanty), had been treated by me for the last few years. She suffered from digestive derangement, and sometimes from violent attacks of Megrim. Thislady awoke one morning with a violent pain in the right upper arm and region of right shoulder, being of a tearing nature. She had walked the previous evening through a damp meadow, getting her feet wet. The pains wore worse if she moved her arm quickly, but easier on moving it very gently. She was therefore keeping it constantly in gentle motion. The parts affected were painful on being touched. During the night perspiration had been excessive, and afterwards made its appearance every morning between two and six o'clock, when the pains were always worse. The patient complained also of a pain in the right hand and powerlessness, which prevented her from lifting anything heavy. She often felt rather exhausted, and had to lie down. I gave-her no less than five remedies, which seemed to suggest themselves, but without success. From the lady's anæmic condition, and partly Dr. Schüssler's recommendation, made me think of iron. I prescribed his own preparation of ***Ferric phosphate,*** as much as would cover a sixpence, to be taken night and morning. The result was that, after taking the medicine for six days, the pains, with their accompanying symptoms, did not return, although soon after this wet weather set in, when she had generally felt her pains to be worse.

REPORT FROM THE ARCHIVES OF MEDICAL MEN OF THE RHINELANDS AND WESTHALIA:-

Dr. Brisken mentions three cases of rheumatic fever. One case was that of a bookbinder, middle aged, whom Dr. Brisken had treated three years previously for this malady. On that occasion his recovery took from eight to ten weeks. The patient was again attacked in the joints of the hands and knees, when he received ***Ferric phosphate*** every hour; and as the fever had abated, ***Potassium chloride*** was given the same way. On the fifth day he was able to return to his work.

The second case was that of a gentleman, aged 70. He had rheumatism in the shoulder and elbow joints. He had been cupped, which made him worse. His joints were wrapped in waldwolle (turpentine wool) with no effect. He had not been in bed the last two nights, as on lying down the pains were worse. On the third day he came under Dr. Brisken's treatment. On the use of ***Ferric phosphate*** the fever ceased in a few days, after which ***Potassium chloride*** was given. In a short time complete recovery resulted.

To a third case Dr. Brisken was called on the eighth day after seizure. All the joints were swollen, and the patient had not been able to stay in bed a single night. In the morning he received ***Potassium chloride*** with such good results that during the next night he was able to stay in bed, and in twelve days was completely cured.

Dr. Orth relates:—Elizabeth F., a widow, aged seventy, consulted me on April 5th, on account of an epithelioma seated on the right cheek, reaching from the eyelid to below the nostril. It was almost circular, and about the size of a florin. The epithelioma had existed for some years, and was at the stage of forming an ulcer, with hard base and callous-edges. I ordered *Potassium sulphate,* a powder every evening, and lint saturated with a lotion made of *Potassium sulphate* for external application, to be changed frequently. On May 6th I noticed that the ulcer had visibly diminished, and on May 23rd, the ulcer had cicatrized to the size of & sixpenny piece. A few days later the lady left to return home, and I regret I have not heard from her since.

William W., a factory worker, came to me on Sept. the 4th. He suffered from epithelioma, which was situated on the right side of the nose, almost immediately below the corner of the eye, and about the size of a two-shilling piece. The eye itself seemed to be sympathetically affected, whether through the irritation of the discharge, which might have found its way into the eye from the edge of the eyelid, which, however, was not greatly destroyed. Be that as it may, there were conjunctivitis palpebrarum and bulbi, with dulness of the cornea. The ulcer at the side of the nose had existed for four years. At first there was a slightly red spot, which was a little raised and swollen. Later on it became covered with a horny-like scab, which after a time fell off and left a sore. This spread slowly, but steadily. The patient had during the whole time of its existence consulted a great number of doctors. He had also been treated for two months by a specialist for the eye, after it had become implicated; but all without effect *Potassium sulphate* was now given him—a dose night and morning; and externally a lotion of *Potassium sulphate* was used. After only a few days the inflammation disappeared. The ulcer began also to heal under the steady treatment. By the 8th of October, the sore had cicatrized so that only a speck was left, when the patient was able to resume work again on the 9th of October.

The following is a case of a lady, aged 44. I saw, writes Dr. A., of Arnsberg, on the 9th of February, a lady suffering from mental derangement. Religious melancholy was at the root, although before this occurrence she had not inclined to religious excitement. She now declared she was lost for ever, lamented, cried, wrung her hands, and tore her clothes, or pieces of paper which were laid about to prevent her tearing her garments. She did not know those around her, and was unable to sleep. Her eyes had an unconscious stare, and frequently it required two people to hold her down. Only by holding her nose and by force, a little food or medicine could be put down her throat. I prescribed *Potassium phosphate,* as her condition, though one of excitement, was originally one of depression, to which *Potassium phosphate* is suited. Dr. Schüssler says in his book:—A functional disturbance of the molecules of this salt causes in the brain mental depression, showing itself in irritability, terror, weeping, nervousness, &c., as well as softening of the brain. She took *Potassium phosphate* with excellent results. A former experience gained by this remedy led me to select it.

On that occasion it was in the case of an old man, aged eighty. He suffered from mental derangement, which showed itself in the form of intense Hypochondriasis and Melancholia. He was tired of life; but had a fear of death. For weeks he had been treated to no purpose with many remedies apparently called for, as Nux vomica, Aur; Bromide of Potassium in allopathic doses. But he was rapidly cured by the continuous use of *Potassium phosphate* Even after eight hours from the commencement of the treatment, a certain feeling of calmness was experienced, and that night he had a quiet sleep. I had, therefore, no reason to regret the treatment I selected, as the improvement continued steadily, so that on the 25th of February I discontinued my professional visits.

I have seen my previous patient frequently, busily engaged in her home with her usual cheerfulness, and she speaks quite calmly of her past illness.

FROM AN ADDRESS GIVEN BY DR. SCHLEGELMAN AT R., 1875.

1. A.S., the child of a post official visiting here, was taken ill with an attack of very slight scarlatina. The rash had disappeared after scarcely twenty-four hours. The throat symptoms, at first threatening to be severe, disappeared in three to four days. On the seventh day almost complete retention of urine set in, as in twenty-four hours only a very small quantity was passed, although the child drank a good deal. The urine contained some albumen, the feet were swollen, the abdomen very much distended. As the child was all this time in high fever, and at night delirious, I advised the parents on my visit on the morning of the eighth day to consult a sec-

ond physician. Dr. Gerstu, who was called in to consult with me, agreed completely with my diagnosis. When I told him that I had not had any results from any of the medicines, such as belladonna, cautharides, and arsenic, we agreed to give *Potassium chloride*—every two hours a small pinch. In the evening the little one was already better. She had passed a tolerable quantity of urine free from albumen; the pulse steadier, the skin moist. The following night the little girl slept quietly for several hours. In the morning almost free from fever, and could be considered convalescent. We continued the use of *Potassium chloride,* and a few days after she was able to return home perfectly well.

2. A boy, W. T., aet 11, had been treated here by Dr. Fuchs for violent inflammation of the bowels. During the course of the disease I had been called in. We had allowed him to return by rail when convalescent to his home at B.A week after he contracted there inflammation of the peritoneum, with high fever and acute pains. My colleague Fuchs and I prognosced the case as rather hopeless, as he had been so much reduced by the disease he had just passed through, being constitutionally delicate. Having found atropine, aconite, etc., as well as strapping, of no avail, we decided upon *Ferric phosphate* as a last resource. A dose of ten to fifteen grains per hour. The effect was a brilliant one. The fever abated; the pains decreased rapidly. This medicine we continued till the fever had quite subsided, and profuse perspirations commenced. At this stage we gave *Potassium chloride,* which caused the absorption of the rather profuse effusion.

3. A very nervous lady, 26 years of age, who suffered continually either from headache, toothache, face ache, and pains in the limbs, or spasms, cramps of the stomach, indigestion, flatulence, and colic, was tormented day and night with a spasmodic cough, suppression of urine, want of sleep, and so on. In short, every day she complained of some trouble or other, and in reality suffered from it. This case almost brought me into despair. All my exertions were in vain. All the best remedies known left me in the lurch. Almost every day a letter or telegram informed me she was getting worse, and summoned me to call. I had the happy thought of looking at Schüssler's book. I found under the head of *Magnesium phosphate* all her symptoms grouped together. I gave her this medicine, and from that moment we both had peace. "The medicine has done me no end of good," she said. And although formerly she had to keep her bed for weeks, she soon after was able to go

into the garden, and later on visited a watering-place. I had to give her, however, plenty of the good remedy before leaving.

4. A young lady of seventeen, M.M., consulted me on account of an obstinate acrid leucorrhea. I tried the whole series of remedies indicated for such cases. All were without effect, so that I could not but wonder at the patience and perseverance of the patient, whom I saw once a week. In this case Schüssler again helped me out of the dilemma *Potassium chloride* effected a quick and permanent cure.

In the year 1875 Dr. Schlegelman reports from Regensburg:—D. A., aged twenty, a delicate lady, who suffered in her childhood a good deal from scrofula, was attacked last winter by a severe pain in the back, in consequence of catching cold. The third to the fifth ribs were very sensitive to pressure. Violent trembling of the right foot, and at the same time of the right arm, set in the moment she attempted to move the arm or extend the hand, and thus made all work impossible. The patient was all the more depressed about this, as in her vocation she had a good deal of writing to do. I gave many remedies—pulsatilla, rhus. tox., belladonna, mix vomica, platina, &c., all without effect. I sent the young lady into the country; her condition remained the same. New remedies had no better results. At last I thought to have found her remedy in zinc, met., as I had heard nothing from her for four weeks. How astonished was I to find my patient, whom I thought cured, entering my consulting room on the 30th Sept. trembling worse than ever.

On my inquiry why she had not called sooner, she told me somewhat timidly she had gone to Mariabrun to see Dr. Bäurin, and used the cure during the time. The result, as I could easily see, had not been successful. Consequently, she placed herself under my treatment again. I told her I was willing to treat her, and opened Schüssler's Therapy. I chose *Magnesium phosphate,* and had no reason to regret ray choice, for after the first few doses (three times a day, ten grains) a decided improvement was noticed, of which I heard on the 11th October, when I saw her again. At this date not even a trace of the trembling could be seen.

She had written repeatedly after this, and even then had experienced no trembling whatever. The cure was complete, as she had up to date been doing all kinds of needlework and a great deal of writing, without any recurrence of the affection.

Dr. Schlegelman writes:—January 1876. I was attacked with rheumatism the latter part of November travelling by rail, sitting close to the window of a draughty carriage. My whole right side was affected going, and on returning the pains were very severe. Especially worse on every movement I made. Bryonia eased me temporarily. I only reached home at midnight, and had a very bad night. Bryonia was of little use now. I applied the electric current next morning repeatedly, but it was of no avail. I then took a pinch of the *Ferric phosphate,* and, as if by magic, the pains disappeared, and did not return.

Dr. Fuchs, of Regensburg, reports:—In August, 1875, I cured a lady 40 years of age, who had suffered for a considerable time from an effusion in bursa of the knee-cap. 12 doses of *Calcium phosphate,* 2 dozes per diem, according to Dr. Schüssler, removed this chronic condition of housemaid's knee.

Dr. Schlegelman reports:— *Potassium sulphate* I have repeatedly tested in wandering rheumatism, and have had very favourable results.

1. L., of Regensburg, a strong healthy man of 26, had taken cold during a state of perspiration, and contracted acute rheumatism of the joints (rheumatic fever). At first the right shoulder was attacked. The patient had violent pains and high fever. Brg., which seemed decidedly indicated here, had no other effect except that the pain on the next morning had changed its seat, and had appeared in the left knee. In this way he continued for several days, under the use of various medicines. Either the one or other of' several joints were affected. The most distressing pains continued day and night, and evidently the patient was greatly reduced. At last I decided to test Schüssler's medicine. I gave *Potassium sulphate* The result was very favourable. The wandering pains ceased changing their location, and the pain confined itself to the right shoulder again, but was far less violent than before. Under the continued use of this medicine, the fever and pains gradually disappeared. Sleep and appetite returned, and no other joints were implicated. Eight days after giving the first dose of *Potassium sulphate,* the patient was dismissed as convalescent. No relapse occurred.

2. I have made little use as yet of Dr. Schüssler's *Potassium phosphate,* but have, notwithstanding, effected a few very interesting cures.

A woman, aged 54, came under my treatment, who had been for many years treated without success. She had taken steel baths, a great many steel pills and drops, and quinine. She complained of severe vertigo felt mostly on rising from a sitting position, and on looking upwards. She was constantly in dread of falling, and did not venture to leave her room. I gave her all the usual remedies without any benefit. At last I gave her, in May 1875, two doses daily of Dr. Schüssler's **Potassium phosphate** I had the pleasure of seeing a rapid and decided cure following this. The patient can attend to her domestic duties; she can go out alone, even to distances, and is almost completely cured of her painful sensation of giddiness.

3. I have hitherto only given **Sodium phosphate** in scrofulous subjects, and only then when my old remedies calci. carb., etc., failed.

One case was particularly striking on account of its being cured so rapidly. In May last a little girl of eight was brought to me who suffered from severe conjunctivitis, with great dread of light. She had been treated for some time by an ordinary practitioner, but without effect. I ascertained that her eye affection dated from the time she had had measles some years previous. Calci. carb. and other medicines proved ineffectual The enlargements of the glands of the neck, and the creamy secretion of the eyelids, led me to try **Sodium phosphate,** of which I administered a dose three times daily. A week later on, the child was brought to me, her eyes being perfectly cured.

4. A landed proprietor, 44 years of age, wrote to me a few weeks ago—"The medicine I have taken very steadily, and for a long time attended strictly to my diet/ In spite of this, my trouble is no better; I may almost say it has become worse."

The conditions were these :— 1. I feel almost constantly a taste as of bile.

2. My tongue is covered with a curdy, bitter coating.

3. During the day, especially after food, I suffer from eructations of gases, which have either a bitter taste or are tasteless.

4. My complexion is rather yellow.

5. The appetite very slight; no thirst. My favourite 'beverage, beer, is distasteful to me.

6. I incline to shiver, and am somewhat faint.

7. My head is but little involved, but feel a constant pressure over one eye.

8. Stools are normal, but scanty, on account of spare diet

The whole condition discloses that I have bile in the stomach. This far the patient's own report. To this I may add that the patient in question had already taken by my orders nux. vom. and pulsatilla. He had used the waters of Marienbad the previous summer on the recommendation of another medical man.

I sent him *Sodium sulphate,* with the request to take daily three doses of this powder. The gentleman came six or seven days later to my consulting room to thank me for the valuable medicine. The powder, he said, has really worked wonders. All my ailments have disappeared as if by magic, and I feel at last perfectly well.

5. I have used *Sodium chloride* repeatedly, and especially in obstinate cases of salivation, with excellent results. One case in particular was cured with remarkable rapidity by this remedy. A young lady, act. 20, who suffered from severe inflammation of the tonsils, so that she could scarcely swallow milk or water, had received from me a preparation of mercury sol.

The inflammation of the tonsils was reduced very quickly, but another evil set in, namely, violent salivation. The gums were loosened, bleeding easily, and standing back from the teeth, and the teeth were slackened.

I thought of curing this affection also with mercury, with which I had often before succeeded in such cases; but by continuing this remedy the evil was only increased. Now I ascertained from the patient that in the previous summer she had been ill at N., and the doctor had given her a good deal of calomel, which caused fearful and long-continued salivation. She was afraid the evil would again become very tedious, as it had been so bad at N. I now stopped the mercury sol., and ordered *Sodium chloride,* a dose the size of a bean every two hours.

The success surpassed my most sanguine expectations. In twenty-four hours the swelling of the glands had distinctly diminished, and in three days a complete cure was effected.

6. D. R., a boy 7 years of age, who took spurious croup whenever there was a sharp, keen north-east wind, having had a few years before a very severe attack of true croup, this past autumn had again an attack, with fever, and a. loud barking cough.

Aconite and liver of sulphur, which have been recommended by so many authors against spurious croup, produced no change whatever, so that I prepared myself, in the case of this boy, for a continuance of the affection, as usual, for several days. The nights especially were very restless, with much coughing, rough and hard, so that his relatives were very anxious. There were dry heat and great oppression present. I exchanged my Hep. sulph. for *Potassium chloride,* and gave every two hours a full dose. After a few doses the cough became loose, lost completely the barking sound, and the whole of the following night my little patient slept quietly, so that on the following morning he awoke able to get up quite recovered.

7. A. R. v. G., a young lady of 18, had visited, along with her mother, in the past summer (1875), a hydropathic establishment. Without being ill, she had used the baths, and even during her period. Immediately after this, she took violent spasms or cramps, which set in daily, and continued, though she returned home. A medical man was consulted, as the disease only increased in spite of the different medicines she took. A second doctor was consulted, who quite agreed in the diagnosis as well as the treatment adopted by his colleague. Injections of morphium, very strong and repeated several times daily, were the main remedies applied, but the distressing ailment could not be removed; oh the contrary, the cramps increased in violence and frequency. The medical, men in attendance finally declared that there was no chance of improvement until the patient would take some steel baths in the spring. The parents were afraid that their daughter would not live to see the spring, and if she did, that she would not be fit to be removed. They, therefore, telegraphed requesting a visit from me.

On the 6th of September last I saw the patient for the first time. I had known her formerly, and was astonished to see, instead of the blooming healthy girl she had been, a pale emaciated figure whom I should not have recognised. During my presence she had an attack; her features were distorted, the eyes turned upwards, froth came to the mouth, and then a fearful paroxysm of beating and striking with the hands and feet, such as I had never seen before. This was only the commencement. Suddenly the trunk of her body was contorted in an indescribable manner; the back of the head pressed deeply into the pillows, the feet forced against the foot of the bed, her chest and abdomen became arched like a bridge, drawn up almost half a yard. In this unnatural position she was suspended several seconds. Suddenly the whole body jerked upwards with a bound, and the poor sufferer was tossed about for some seconds, with her spine contracted.

During the whole attack, which lasted several minutes, she was quite unconscious; pinching and slapping had no effect; dashing cold water in the face, or applying burnt feathers to the nostril, were ineffectual; the pupils were quite insensible to light

Ignatia, which I ordered, had no effect; cupr. metal. acted better, but only temporarily; Belladonna, Ipec, and Pulsatilla (the latter for suppressed catamenia), were of no use. The attacks did not increase, neither did they decrease in the least degree. The morphium injections too were continued at the desire of her friends.

When at my visit on the 4th of October, the spasms came on again with such violence that the bedstead gave way, I consulted Schüssler's Therapy, and ordered *Magnesium phosphate.*

After taking this remedy on the 10th of October, the catamenia appeared; but her condition otherwise was in no way changed. The spasms continued with the same violence. Then remembering Schüssler's injunction to use *Calcium phosphate* where *Magnesium phosphate,* though indicated by the symptoms, proves ineffectual, I gave her *Calcium phosphate* on the 16th of October, a full doze every two hours. Immediately the spasms became less frequent. On the sixth day there was an attack, weak and of short duration. From this date she had peace until the 6th of November, the day of the return of the catamenia, which was preceded by a short slight attack.

On the 14th of December I had a call from the young lady, looking well and blooming, who wished to consult me for a slight bronchial affection. She told me that she was completely cured of her attacks, and that at the beginning of December she had been quite regular, without experiencing any inconvenience.

7. Dr. S. writes:—Mrs. S., aged 24, of Regensburg, who had been suffering for several years from lichen (skin affection) had used various well-known medicines which had done her no good. I tried various remedies, and at last cured her. A few months ago she came again, and the lichen was worse than ever. My former remedy had no effect; and with several others, arsenic, &c, it was no better. I gave her *Calcium sulphate* night and morning, in quantities as large as a bean, and in a fortnight the cure was completed.

8. Silica has proved an excellent remedy. Within the-last few months I was able to cure a young lady, 16 years-old, who lives in the country. I did not see her myself. The mother of the girl came to me almost crying, and told me her daughter had been suffering for the last few months-from her right foot. The medical men treating her there-declared that the foot, must be amputated. It was fearfully swollen; the discharge of matter was excessive; her leg was almost bent to a right angle at the knee-joint, and could absolutely not be stretched out, I advised her to give up

the internal, as well as the external remedies, and gave her **Silica** to be taken once daily. Three months later the-patient came herself, walking without any assistance. The foot was almost completely healed, with only a slight discharge of matter,

Thus I succeeded, also, in a case of discharge from the ear, which had been treated for a long time ineffectually, and had caused the patient severe pain day and nights. This case also was cured with **Silica.**

From the Rundschau:—Magnesium phosphate6 for Hooping Cough. In the spring of 1881, when there was an epidemic of hopping cough amongst the children here, a little child of ten months was given up by the family doctor. I heard this from the father of the child, who was in great grief. He mentioned that the spasms, which occurred about ten times in the course of the day, were so severe that the little face became quite livid, blue, and swollen. I at once gave **Magnesium phosphate.6** One single powder moderated the spasms so forcibly that they returned only occasionally, and the attacks were quite mild. Five days later I gave some **Potassium phosphate,** but without beneficial effect, then **Calcium phosphate,** and it had no good effect, as the paroxysms grew only worse for want of **Magnesium phosphate** I ordered it to be taken again, and in a very short time the spasms and hoop were gone, and the child recovered rapidly.

A FEW CASES FROM THE AUTHOR'S PRACTIVE:—

February, 1880:—In a village a few miles from the town of Oldenburg a child was taken ill with Diphtheria, which at an early stage was complicated by an affection of the larynx. The child was treated by the ordinary methods; and died. Almost at the same time a child of another family in the village was attacked by Diphtheria with the same complication. The father of the latter child came to me. I gave **Potassium chloride** for the disease in the first instance, and **Calcium phosphate** for the affection of the larynx, to be taken alternately. I requested the father to inform me without fail of the result, which he promised to do. Two days after, I received a letter from him, in which he informed me that the child had completely recovered.

October, 1879.—Treatment of the bite of insects.—Moisten the parts affected with a little water; put a small quantity of **Sodium chloride** upon it, and rub it in with a rotatory motion of the finger. The pain ceases almost instantly on this manipulation.

I was consulted by the relatives of a man suffering from ***delirium tremens*** I ordered ***Sodium chloride*** A complete cure followed speedily.

Sodium chloride is the true remedy, as ***delirium tremens*** is caused by a disturbance of the balance of the molecules of the Sodium chloride and molecules of water in some portion of the brain.

A young man complained of an unnatural appetite. He-declared that almost every hour he felt the need of taking food at the same time he felt exhausted and languid. There were no secondary symptoms present. The tongue was-clean, the urine was not increased, evacuations normal. ***Potassium phosphate*** cured the patient in the course of two-days.

A lady felt for two days a drawing laming pain in the sole of her foot. The affected spot, about the size of a florin, had a bluish appearance. Pressure, or a blow, or other mechanical influences, had not preceded it. A dose of ***Potassium phosphate*** subdued the pain in about half an hour.

An old lady had become bedridden for the last fortnight on account of the following ailment. She felt a considerable pain in the lower part of the thorax on the left side, which increased when she coughed. The cough was a slightly catarrhal one. The invalid felt very exhausted, and had no appetite. The tongue was dry, the pulse frequent, weak, and intermittent. ***Potassium phosphate*** cured her in the space of a week.

To the above I add another important effect of ***Potassium phosphate*** By the use of it, spurious labour pains subside, weak pains are stimulated by it, and often in the shortest space of time the desired effects are produced with most favourable results.

H. W. SCHÜSSLER.

THERAPEUTICAL INDEX.

The Inorganic Cell-Salts.

The Tissue Cell-Salts as specially prepared for DR. SCHÜSSLER *act as* MO-LECULAR-CELLULAR THERAPEUTICS.

Modern English Terms.	*Terms as used in German.*
I. Calcium phosphate.	1. Calcarea phosphorica.
II. Calcium sulphate.	2. Calcarea sulphurica.
III. Calcium fluoride.	3. Calcium fluorica.
IV. Ferric phosphate.	4. Ferrum phosphoricum.
V. Potassium chloride.	5. Chlorkalium.
VI. Potassium phosphate.	6. Kali phosphoricum.
VII. Potassium sulphate.	7. Kali sulphuricum.
VIII. Magnesium phosphate.	8. Magnesia phosphorica.
IX. Sodium chloride.	9. Natrum muriaticum.
X. Sodium phosphate.	10. Natrum phosphoricum.
XI. Sodium sulphate.	11. Natrum sulphuricum.
XII. Silica.	12. Silicea.

DIRECTIONS.

THE DOSE.—Dissolve from 3 to 5 grains of the powder, (a quantity about the size of a pea,) in, say, a table or tea spoonful of water for a single dose. For convenience take as much powder as will lie on a sixpenny piece, dissolve it in a cupful of water, and make 6 to 8 doses or sips of this quantity. In the case of Magnesium phosphate, where warmth is agreeable and soothing, *hot* water may be advantageously taken.

If from any reason the patient cannot readily take the remedy in water, the powder may be taken dry upon the tongue, though this is not the preferable or most effective way.

TIME.—A dose should be taken every hour, or even oftener if the case be very acute. In less urgent cases, a dose every 2 hours. In chronic cases 4 doses daily.

ALTERNATION.—When two remedies have to be taken alternately, each must be kept in a separate cup, the one to be taken in turns or time about with the other.

THE INTERCURRENT REMEDY.—To be taken occasionally, between or in place of the chief or principal remedy or remedies, such as *Ferric phosphate,* in any disease, as symptoms-may arise in complications. For *chronic* cases, the *intercur-rent,* such as *Calcium phosphate,* a dose every day, night and morning, or only every second day.

EXTERNAL APPLICATION.—The remedies must always-be accompanied by it internally. Dissolve a good pinch of the powder prescribed in half a tumblerful of water. This lotion can be used tepid or cold as may be required or preferred, for bathing the parts with; or, if to be applied on lint as a compress, with oilskin over it; or a poultice may be moistened with it, though a compress is preferable to it. It may be used as a gargle. Wetted and mixed with Olive Oil or Glycerine or Vaseline it may be applied like ointment, or the parts may simply be moistened with the lotion as often as desirable under existing circumstances. Any of these ways of application maybe adopted whenever *external use* is prescribed.

THE TONGUE and its appearance in disease forms a very important index as a rule to the remedy required. Different salts when deficient in function, cause a peculiar appearance of the tongue (for which consult page 63).—The best time to examine the tongue is *before* and not after meals.

1.—Calcium Phosphate.

The Diseases forming this group must be healed or treated with *Calcium phos-phate,* as they have their seat either in the bone, connective-tissue, or blood-cells. The *Calcium phosphate* has a chemical affinity for albumen, which forms the or-ganic basis-for this salt in the tissue-cells.

All Ailments that are obstinate and do not yield to its own remedy may require a few doses of *Calcium phosphate* More particularly is this required with growing young people or old persons.

Albumenuria—Albumenous urine calls for the use of this cell-salt as an intercurrent remedy.

Anœmia (poverty of red blood)—To supply new blood cells, this. salt as first remedy.

Bone diseases, see also Rickets.

Bones broken, surgical aid is necessary, and for the uniting of the fractured ends this cell-salt is beneficial.

Bones, soft, weakly.

Bowed legs in children, to strengthen the weak bones.

Bright's disease (of the kidneys) for the albumen; as an intercurrent remedy.

Cancer, in scrofulous constitutions.

Catarrhs, chronic, of anæmic persons; as an intercurrent remedy.

Chlorosis ("green sickness") of young females.

Clergyman's sore throat; as an intercurrent remedy.

Constitutional weakness; as a tonic for delicate persons.

Consumption, in, to lessen the emaciation.

Convalescence, during; after acute diseases.

Convulsions, from teething, without fever, if Mag. phos. fails.

Cough, in consumption; as an intercurrent remedy.

Deficient development of young people, stunted growth.

Delicacy in growing girls and boys, delicate pale appearance when breeding second teeth.

Delicate young infants are much benefitted by the use of this constitutional remedy.

Dropsy, from non-assimilation, or anæmia.

Eczema, with anæmia (bloodlessness); as an intercurrent remedy.

Enuresis, nocturnal, from general weakness.

Eyelids, spasmodic affection, if Mag. phos. fails.

Emaciation, without very special ailments.

Face-ache (neuralgic, rheumatic), commences or is worst at night.

Fits, during development in childhood, youth, or old age, where the lime salts are at fault.

Fits, in the strumous and scrofulous.

Fontanelles, remaining open too long.

Fractured bones, to promote union.

Freckles are generally lessened by it, and the constitutional want of this salt corrected.

Gall-stones, to prevent re-formation of new ones.

Glands, enlarged, chronic; as intercurrent remedy.

Gonorrhœa, with anæmia.

Gout, rheumatic, worse at night and with the changes of the weather.

Gravel, for the calculous, gritty deposit in urine.

Gums, painful in teething children, and if inflamed, alternate doses of this cell-salt and Ferric phosphate.

Hœmorrhoids, chronic, in anæmic or weakly patients; intercurrently with Calcium fluoride.

Headache, a cold feeling in the head, and the head *feels* cold to the touch; also Magnesium phos.

Hernia (rupture) in anæmic patients; as an intercurrent remedy.

Hip-joint disease, when there is ulceration of bone.

Hooping-cough, in weakly constitutions, or in teething children, and obstinate cases; as an intercurrent remedy.

Housemaid's knee, chronic, with anæmia.

Hydrocele, if Sod. chlor. fails.

Hydrocephalus, water in the head, acute and chronic; chief remedy.

Inflammation of the eyes, dry, during dentition; intercurrently with Ferric phos.

Intestinal worms, predisposition to, in anæmic patients.

Intermittent fever, chronic, of children.

Kidney disease, with albumen in the urine; also Potass, chlor.

Lameness, rheumatic, obstinate; intercurrently with Potass, chloride.

Leucorrhœa ("Whites"); as a constitutional tonic, and intercurrent remedy, with the chief remedy.

Lumbago; alternately with Ferric phos.

Lupus, if a partial manifestation of scrofulosis; see also Potass, chlor.

Neuralgia, commencing at night, or periodically worse at night. See also Magnesium phosphate.

Ozœna, *with scrofulous symptoms.*

Pains, *generally when heat or cold make the ailment worse.*

Pains (rheumatic) in the head, worst during the night.

Pains in the head, worse with heat or cold.

Pains which are worse in the night require this salt intercurrently with the other remedies specially called for.

Perspiration too frequent or excessive, especially if perspiring too-much about the head.

Rheumatism, which is worst at night.

Rheumatism, aggravated with heat or cold.

Rheumatism, worse in bad weather.

Rheumatism, worse with change of weather.

Rheumatism, chronic, of the joints, with cold or numb feeling.

Rickets in delicate children, caused by soft sponginess of bone, from want of the phosphate of lime molecules.

Skin affections of anæmic persons; as intercurrent remedy.

Spinal curvature; also mechanical supports.

Spinal weakness.

Stone in the bladder, to check re-formation of the same; buttermilk as a dietary help.

Suppurations of true bone.

Teeth, too rapid decay of.

Teething disorders; as chief remedy.

Teething too late.

Teething troublesome, little ailments caused by it.

Tonsils, chronic swelling; as an intercurrent remedy.

Toothache, worse at night, or worse with hot or cold fluids.

Toothache, always worse in bad weather; as an intercurrent remedy.

Tubercles of the skin.

Typhoid fever. As the disease declines this remedy will act as a restorative.

Ulceration of bone substance (true bone).

2.—Calcium Sulphate.

The Diseases forming this group must be healed or treated with **Calcium sulphate,** as it is curative in suppurations—those suppurations which arise **around** the connective tissue (superficial).

All Ailments which are connected with swelling of soft parts and threaten to suppurate, or are discharging pus (matter) and blood.

Abscess, this remedy will shorten the suppurative process, and bring forward the pus if any has to come. If the abscess be treated with this salt and **Potassium chloride** alternately, it may be blighted, and much suffering spared. See also Silica.

Boils; as third remedy, to reduce and control suppuration as above.

Bruises, when neglected and are threatening to suppurate.

Bubo, to control suppuration, in alternation with Potass, chloride.

Burns and scalds, *which are suppurating; as second remedy.*

Carbuncles, *to control the formation of pus. See also Silica and Potass, chloride.*

Chilblains, *after Potassium chloride, or when taken up in a suppurating stage.*

Consumption.

Cornea, *abscess of, deep-seated; also Silica.*

Crusta lactea, *"scald head" of children, after Potass, chlor. if there is mattery discharge,*

Cuts, *suppurative, to control suppuration; lumpy bloody matter.*

Deafness, *when connected with discharge of matter from the ear, not yielding to Silica.*

Diarrhœa, *mattery, bloody-mattery.*

Dropsy, *post-scarlatinal, after Sodium chloride and Sodium sulphate when matter forms in rare cases.*

Dysentery, *mattery bloody stools.*

Ears, *discharge of matter and blood. See under Silica.*

Empyœma, *pus forming in cavity of lung, or pleura.*

Expectoration *of purulent bloody matter.*

Exudations, *oozing of matter on the skin, or on internal serous surfaces.*

Eyes, *inflammation of, with discharge of thick yellow matter; or Silica.*

Festers (common term for suppurations), are generally cured by this remedy. See also Silica.

Furuncles (boils), when pus forms.

Gathered finger, for the last stage when matter forms; externally also on lint; when the nail is implicated, also Silica.

Glands, lymphatic, threatening suppuration, and during discharge of pus. See also Silica.

Gonorrhœa, *in suppurating stage.*

Hypopion, *to absorb the effusion of pus.*

Injuries (from accidents), neglected cuts, wounds, bruises, if suppurating.

Mastitis, gathered breasts; a third remedy to prevent matter forming; with Potass, chloride.

Mastitis, "Weed," gathered breast after the use of Potass, chloride, and on lint to absorb the matter, or if discharging, to shorten the process: also Silica. If there is persistent hardness, Calcium fluoride.

Pimples, if matter forms on the heads of these.

Pustules, nodules, when suppurating.

Quincy, if ulcers form with yellow heads.

Scabs, mattery, forming on heads of nodules and pimples.

Skin affections, scalded head of children, where Potass, chloride does not suffice.

Skin affections, with greenish, brownish, or yellowish scabs; after Potass, chlor.

Skin, suppuration of, after inflammation.

Sores, if matter discharges (pure pus); unhealthy matter, with heavy odour, may require Potass. phosphate as intercurrent remedy.

Suppuration, articular (of the joints); also Silica.

Suppurations, having their seat around the connective-tissue, not of the connective-tissue channels, such as ligaments and fascia.

Swelling of the cheek, after Potass, chlor., if suppuration threatens.

Syphilis, chronic, third stage.

Throat, sore, threatening suppuration.

Throat, ulcerated, when yellow matter forms, last or suppurating stage.

Tonsilitis, last stage, when matter threatens, or has formed on the tonsils.

Ulceration of Glands. If matter is suspected, this remedy and Silica will assist the absorption, or if matter is present it will cleanse and heal the sore. Externally also on lint. The scar left will be very insignificant if treated in this way.

Ulcers, open mattering sores, which may result from abrasions, pimples, wounds, burns, scalds, or bruises.

Ulcers, of lower limbs; if thick yellow matter forms, Silica.

Whitlow, when matter forms; also Silica, for the nail.

Wounds, suppurating; if very thick yellow matter forms, also Silica.

3.—Calcium Fluoride.

The Diseases of this group must be healed or treated with *Calcium fluoride,* as they have their seat in the substance forming the surface of bone, enamel of teeth, and part of all elastic fibres, whether of the epidermis, the connective-tissues, or of the walls of the blood-vessels.

All Ailments which can be traced to relaxed conditions of any of the elastic fibres, including dilatation of blood-vessels, arterial and venous blood tumours, incised tumours and piles, and those also which arise from a disturbed balance of the molecules forming the enamel of teeth and of bone surface.

After-pains, if too weak, contrations too feeble.

Anuerism, at an early stage may be reduced or kept in check with the use of Ferric phosphate and this, as the chief remedies, provided that Iodide of Potass, has not been taken.

Arthritis, gout, with hard swellings and deposit; see also Silica.

Back-ache, simulating spinal irritation.

Back-ache, weak back with dragging pain, down-bearing.

Back, pain in the lower part of the back (sacrum), with a sensation of fulness and burning pain.

Bruises on the surface of the bone, the shin, etc., with lumps, thickening under the periosteum.

Catamenia, excessive, with bearing-down pains.

Cephalhœmatoma, *blood-tumours on the parietal bones of new-born infants, on a rough, bony base.*

Cornea, *opacities, spots on the eye.*

Cough, *with whitish expectoration of tenacious mucus, if Potassium chloride alone is not quite sufficient.*

Dilatation *of blood-vessels; chief remedy to restore the contractility to the elastic fibres.*

Cough, *of heart.*

Displacement *of uterus.*

Dragging pains *in the region of the uterus, and in the thighs.*

Eczema; alternately with Potassium chloride, if the [latter does not suffice.

Enamel of teeth, deficient.

Exudations on the bone surface, hard, rugged (corrugated), pointed elevations.

Flooding; to tone up the contractile power of the uterus.

Ganglion, round swellings or incised tumours, such as on the back of the wrist, from strain of the elastic fibres.

Gout, with hard knotty deposit.

Gouty enlargements of the joints of the fingers.

Growths, small hard lumps seated on the cheek bone or other bony surfaces, if arising from an injury or a bruise; outward application if desirable.

Hœmorrhoids. *See Piles.*

Hip-joint disease, *when the bone is implicated.*

Knots, *hard kernels in the female breast.*

Ozœna, *affection of the nose. See also Potassium phosphate.*

Piles, *bleeding; alternately with such remedies as are specially indicated by the blood and coating of the tongue.*

Piles, *internal or blind, frequently with a pain in the back, generally far down on the sacrum; note the appearance of the tongue, etc., indicating the alternating remedy.*

Piles, *with pressure of blood to the head; Ferric phosphate alternately.*

Prolapsus uteri, *falling or bearing down of uterus.*

Psoriasis, *scaly skin affection, more frequently occurring in middle-aged persons of weak constitution.*

Relaxed condition *of elastic fibres in general.*

Relaxed throat, *with tickling in the larynx, when caused by elongation of uvula.*

Suppuration, *where substance of the bone surface is implicated.*

Swellings, *hard, having their seat in fascia and capsular ligaments, or on tendons.*

Swelling, *hard, on the jaw-bone.*

Testicles, *induration of.*

Tumours, *hard, such as are met with as hard lumps in the female breast.*

Tumours, *vascular, with dilated blood-vessels; chief remedy.*

Ulcerations of bone (bone surface, enamel).

Uvula, relaxed; also Ferric phosphate, and if there is much saliva, Sodium chloride.

Varicose ulceration of veins; also as a lotion on lint Calcium sulphate may also be required.

Varicose veins; this salt as chief remedy internally, and also externally as lotion on lint.

Vomiting of undigested food, if Ferric phosphate does not suffice.

Whitlow, gathered finger, also lotion on lint; if deep-seated and the bone is implicated, see also Silica.

4.—Ferric Phosphate.

The Diseases forming this group must be healed or treated with *Ferric phos-*

phate, as they have their seat in the red blood corpuscles or in the vascular system, *i.e.* in the muscular fibres which are circularly arranged around the walls of the blood vessels.

All Ailments arising from a disturbed circulation, or abnormal condition. (deficiency) of red blood corpuscles. These include all febrile conditions or disturbances of the vascular system, and all inflammations, congestions, and irritations caused by local stasis, *i.e.,* accumulation of blood, through a relaxed condition of the muscular fibres of the walls of the blood-vessels.

Ailments of an inflammatory or congestive nature. The inflammatory stage is recognised by being attended either by heat, pain, redness, irritation, throbbing, fever, or quickened pulse. The tongue is generally red, or with a red line along the centre. If there is a deposit, Ferric phosphate has then to be given in alternation with the remedy selected for the coating of the tongue.

Abscess, the first remedy, to reduce fever, heat, throbbing, pain, and congestion (or excess of blood) in the parts.

Anœmia, *blood poverty, want of red blood; after Calcium phosphate-give this remedy to colour the new blood-cells red, and enrich them.*

Anuerism, *to establish normal circulation, and remove those complications arising from excessive action of the heart, and should be early-resorted to. See Calcium fluoride.*

Articular rheumatism (in the joints), frequent doses at the commencement; and as intercurrent remedy.

Back-ache, pains in the loins, rheumatism.

Bleeding from wounds, Ferric phosphate internally and externally surgical aid if severe.

Bleeding of the nose, whether from injury or otherwise; this generally suffices for children.

Blood, loss of, if bright red and coagulating readily.

Blood, rush of, to the head.

Blows or falls, this remedy internally and externally as speedily as possible.

Boils, at the commencement to reduce heat, blood accumulation, pain and throbbing.

Breathing, short, oppressed, and hurried, at the beginning or during the course of an ailment, accompanied by heat and feverishness.

Bright's disease, when feverishness is present

Bronchial irritation, with heat or burning soreness; any expectoration or secretion will require its special alternating remedy.

Bronchitis, in chronic; occasionally to be taken when a fresh aggravation sets in, or in alternation with the remedy indicated by the expectoration. See page 70.

Bronchitis, inflammatory stage; and after exudation takes place, see remedies, page 70.

Bruises, first remedy; see external use, page 126.

Bubo, with heat, throbbing, or feverishness.

Carbuncles, where there exists feverishness, heat, or throbbing; to reduce the swelling, Potassium chloride.

Catarrh, bronchial; the intercurrent remedy, to be used for inflammatory irritation.

Cheek, swollen, to relieve the pain, congestion, throbbing, and heat; first remedy.

Cholera, if inflammatory in the first stage.

Cold in the head, first stage; for the circulatory disturbance.

Colds, chills, and initiatory stage of most diseases; chief remedy.

Congestions of any organ or part of the body yield to this remedy, as it tones up the blood-vessels, dispels the excess of blood in those parts, and relieves the tension.

Constipation, with heat in the lower bowels.

Convulsions (fits), with fever, of teething children.

Cornea, abscess on, of the eye, for the heat, pain, or redness, first stage; and as intercurrent remedy.

Cough, acute, painful, short tickling; also Calcium fluoride.

Cough, at the commencement.

Cough, from irritation of the windpipe.

Cough, short, sore, or tickling from irritation of the windpipe.

Cough, hard, dry, with soreness.

Cough, very painful, short, spasmodic. In true spasmodic use Magnesium phosphate.

Cough, with a feeling of soreness of lungs.

Croup, if it commences with violent fever; alternately with Potass, chlor.

Cuts; chief remedy internally, and the dressing to be saturated with the lotion. See page 126.

Cystitis (inflammation of the bladder), first stage, with heat, pain, or feverishness.

Deafness from inflammatory action or suppuration, when there is pain, tension, throbbing, or heat.

Diabetes, when there is a quickened pulse, or when there exists pain, heat, or congestion in any part of the system.

Diarrhœa, *from relaxed state of villi or absorbants of the intestines.*

Diarrhœa, *stools of undigested food.*

Dilatation *of heart, or of blood-vessels; in alternation with Calcium fluoride, the chief remedy.*

Diphtheria; *as alternate remedy, at the commencement of the disease, this will lessen the fever. See Potassium chloride.*

Diseases of any kind, if ushered in by rigors (shivers), or heat, accompanied by fever, with quickened puke, or pain; for any or all of these symptoms when they occur.

Dropsy, from loss of blood or fluids; as second remedy, after Calcium phosphate.

Dysentery, if beginning with much fever; as intercurrent remedy.

Dysmenorrhœa, *with hot, flushed face and quick pulse.*

Dysmenorrhœa, *with vomiting of undigested food, sometimes tasting acid.*

Dyspepsia, *with flushed, hot face; epigastrium tender to touch. If there is a coating on the tongue, see page 63.*

Dyspepsia, *indigestion with beating or throbbing, pain, heat, redness or flushing of face, or vomiting of undigested food, the tongue being clean.*

Ear-ache, inflammatory (from cold), with burning or throbbing pain.

Epilepsy (fits), with blood rushing to the head, or with palpitation.

Epistaxis (bleeding of the nose), generally in children, this suffices; if from nervous debility, Potassium phosphate.

Erysipelas, "rose," and erysipelatous inflammations of the skin, for the fever and pain. See page 73.

Eyes, inflammation of, with acute pain, without secretions of mucus or pus. For the latter, see page 61.

Eyes, inflammation of, inflamed, with burning sensation.

Face-ache, with flushing and heat.

Face-ache, worse on moving, with throbbing or pressing pain.

Festers, gatherings, to relieve heat, pain, congestion, and inflammation, first stage.

Feverishness in all its various degrees is met by this salt.

Feverish state, at the commencement or during the course of any disease, calls for the use of this remedy alone, or in alternation with such remedies as co-existing symptoms may require.

Fevers, all, require Ferric phosphate alone, or in alternation with those remedies which the accompanying symptoms require.

Finger, inflamed or painful.

Flatulence, bringing back the taste of food partaken of.

Flushed face, accompanied by headache or fulness in the head.

Flushed face, when a precursor of recurring headaches.

Flushed face, when accompanying a sensation of coldness in nape of neck.

Fractures; (besides mechanical aid) to meet the accompanying injuries to the soft parts, first remedy.

Gastritis (inflammation of the stomach), with much pain, swelling, tenderness of pit of stomach, especially if vomiting of food occurs.

Giddiness (vertigo), from rush of blood to the head, with flushing, throbbing, or pressing pain.

Hœmorrhage (bleeding, loss of blood), if bright red, with tendency to coagulation.

Hœmorrhoids (piles), inflamed; alternately with Calcium fluoride, the chief remedy; and as lotion, cold, externally.

Hœmorrhoids *bleeding piles, blood bright red, tendency to form a thickened soft mass.*

Headache, *pains which are worse on stooping and moving.*

Headache, *with vomiting of. undigested food.*

Headache, *congestive, with pressing or stitching pain, and soreness to the touch; pressing a cold object against the spot seems to ease the pain. If there is also a furred tongue. See page 63.*

Headache, *of children generally requires this remedy only.*

Headache, *with a throbbing sensation.*

Headache, *with red face and suffused redness of the eyes.*

Headache, *sick, with vomiting of food as taken, undigested.*

Heat and feverishness *at the beginning of any disease or ailment.*

Hip-joint disease; *for the inflammation of the soft parts, pain, throbbing and heat.*

Hoarseness, *painful, of singers or speakers, from over-exertion of voice.*

Hooping cough, *with vomiting of food; for the hoop or spasm, Magnesium phosphate.*

Hyperœmia; blood accumulated in any of the blood-vessels (Stasis). Cause: want of proper balance of the iron-molecules in the *muscular fibres,* which are circularly arranged around these vessels; thus relaxed they lose their tonicity, and do not support normal circulation.

Incontinence of urine, if from weakness of the sphincter muscle.

Indigestion, from relaxed condition of the muscular fibres of the blood vessels of the stomach, with burning, tenderness, pain on pressure, or flushed face and pain after taking food.

Inflammation of the skin, with or without much fever, heat, pain, throbbing and redness.

Inflammations, all, as well as all congestions and irritations; they are caused by excess of blood in the blood vessels, or in the capillaries of any of the tisanes. They require first Ferric phosphate, and Potassium chloride as second remedy. Such are:—

Bronchitis, inflammation of the Bronchi (windpipe).
Carditis,   „   heart
Cerebritis,   „   brain.
Cystitis,   „   bladder.
Duodenitis,   „   duodenum.
Encephalitis, „   membrane covering the brain.
Enteritis, „   intestines (bowels).
Gastritis, „   stomach.

Hepatitis, inflammations of the liver.
Laryngitis,   „   larynx.
Meningitis,   „   cerebro spinal membrane
Mastitis,   „   breasts, commonly called "weed."
Metritis, „   uterus (womb).
Nephritis,   „   kidneys.
Otitis,   „   ear.
Pericarditis,   „   sac enclosing the heart.
Peritonitis,   „   membrane lining the belly;
                 also called inflammation of the side.
Periostitis,   „   periosteum, or membrane covering all bone.
Phlebitis, „   veins.
Phrenitis,„   brain, or brain fever.
Pneumonia,   „   lungs.
Pleuritis, „   pleura, covering of the lung, also called Pleurisy.
Stomatitis,   „   mouth.
Spleenitis,   „   spleen.
Synovitis,„   synovial membrane.
Tonsilitis,„   tonsils.
Tympanitis,   „   drum of the ear.

Injuries, cuts, fresh wounds; this remedy prevents pain, congestion, swelling, or feverishness. Use also external applications. Surgical aid if severe.

Intermittent fever, with vomiting of food.

Irritations of throat, or other parts, with redness or heat.

Ischuria, suppression of urine, of recent date, with heat; also for little children.

Lameness, rheumatic, with feverish symptoms.

Lungs, inflammation of; first stage, until free perspiration is established, and until health is restored. For expectoration, see page 71.

Lungs, congestion of, with debility and oppression.

Measles, in all stages; and the symptoms of inflammatory affections of chest, eyes, or ears.

Menstruation (monthly period), excessive congestion, blood bright red; this remedy must be taken as a preventative before the periods, if these symptoms are recurrent.

Morning sickness in pregnancy, with vomiting of food as taken; with or without acid taste the food returns undigested.

Mucous membrane, irritation of, with redness, or heat, or dryness.

Neuralgia, congestive or inflammatory, from cold, with pain as if a nail were being driven in; blinding pain, one sided in the head, temples, or over the eye; or in the jaw bone. If this does not suffice, Magnesium phosphate.

Ostitis, with painful and inflamed surrounding soft parts.

Pain of any kind, if accompanied by flushed face, burning or diffused heat.

Pain soreness in every part of the body, especially the joints.

Palpitation of the heart. See also Potassium phosphate.

Periostitis, with painful, inflamed soft parts.

Pimples; for the redness, heat, or congestion of the skin.

Pleurisy; for the fever, pain, stitch in the side, catch in the breath, and short cough; when these abate, Potassium chloride second remedy.

Pleuro-Pneumonia; the principal remedy at first; to be followed by Potassium chloride, or other remedy according to the appearance of the tongue, etc.

Polyuria simplex, excessive secretion of urine.

Quinsy; at first alone, then alternately, with Potassium chloride, or Calcium sulphate.

Retinitis, in the first stage.

Rheumatic fever. This remedy is often the only one required if taken at once; if the swelling be considerable, see Potassium chloride.

Rheumatism, acute articular, very painful; being an inflammatory ferbile disease in first stage.

Rheumatism, acute, when any movement seta up the pain, and all movements tend to keep up or increase the pain.

Rheumatism, of the joints, when painful on moving; first remedy.

Rheumatism, pain felt only during motion, or caused by motion.

Rheumatism, muscular, acute or sub-acute, worse on moving.

Scarlet fever, if the pulse be very high; this as an intercurrent remedy, or in alternation with Potassium chloride.

Skin affections, in the first or inflammatory stage.

Skin affections, inflamed, sore and painful. Sore throat. See throat. See throat.

Sores, to reduce heat, pain and congestion of the parts.

Sprains; to be used as soon as possible externally and internally.

Stiff neck, if simply from a chill.

Stomach-ache, from cold or chill, frequent occurrence in children.

Stomach-ache, inflammatory, if pressure aggravates the pains.

Stomach-ache, with loose evacuations caused by insufficient absorption of moisture, from relaxed condition of villi.

Strains of tendons or ligaments; this salt alternately with Calcium fluoride, the chief remedy.

Teething, with feverishness.

Thread worms.

Throat, ulcerated; this remedy reduces congestion, heat, fever, pain, and throbbing.

Throat, sore, dry, red, inflamed; with much pain.

Throbbing pulsations in any part of the body with or without pain.

Tic-dovloureux, congestive or inflammatory, in which the pain is beating, or stitching with burning soreness, and often pressing and intolerable. If not yielding use also Magnesium phosphate.

Tinnitus aurium (noises in the head), when from excessive flow of blood to the head.

Tongue, inflammation of, dark red, with much swelling; also Potassium chloride.

Toothache, with hot cheek, inflamed gum or root of tooth.

Toothache, worse with hot, better with cold, liquids.

Typhus, in the first stage, to subdue the fever, and regulate the pulse.

Ulceration of glands, to relieve the throbbing pain, soreness, redness, heat, and congested condition; for swelling, Potassium chloride.

Ulcers; if there is fever or heat, redness and congestion of parts, at any stage.

Uterus, inflammation of, first stage, to remove the fever and pain.

Uvula, relaxed, for surrounding parts, if inflamed.

Vaginismus.

Vomiting of undigested food (not mucus) with acid taste.

Vomiting of blood, bright red blood, with tendency to form a gelatinous (liver-like) mass.

Vomiting of undigested food.

Windpipe, irritation of, with burning of the throat, pain and soreness.

Wounds, if severe, surgical aid and Ferr. phos., externally and internally.

Worms, intestinal; predisposition to thread worms.

5.—Potassium Chloride.

The Diseases forming this group must be healed or treated with this cell-salt Fibrinous exudations, glandular infiltration, and inflammatory infiltration of the skin causing swelling of the part, arising from a disturbed balance of the organic (albuminoid) basis in the cells and of the molecules of Potassium chloride or muscle salt, which stands in biological relation to the albuminoid substances—*i.e.,* fibrine. Diseases which arise from a want of this salt are marked either by exudations (swellings), torpor of liver, or by the casting off of effete albuminoid substance, as seen in a white coating of tongue, or whitish secretions and expectorations, which call for the use of Potassium chloride.

All Ailments which have as a principal symptom a *white or gray coating* or fur at the back of the tongue (deposit); *exudation* of a white or gray substance on the mucous lining, tonsils, &c., *swellings* caused by interstitial plastic exudations; *discharges* or *expectoration* of a thick white, or yellowish white, slimy mucus or phlegm from any of the mucous membranes.

Abscess, second stage, or when swelling (interstitial exudation) takes-place.

Adhesions, recent, consequent on inflammations, fibrinous exudations arising from excessive blood pressure on the walls of the blood-vessels.

Aphthœ, *thrush of little children or nursing mothers, without great flow of saliva.*

Articular rheumatism, *acute, for the swelling, or grayish-white coated tongue; in alternation with, or after Ferric phosphate.*

Ascarides, *thread worms.*

Asthma; *for the mucus, if white and hard to cough up, and tongue whitish or furred grayish; for the nervous depression, Potassium phosphate alternately.*

Asthma; *bronchial, treatment as above.*

Bleeding, *when the blood is dark, black, dotted, or tough.*

Blisters, *arising from burns ; also lotion on lint externally.*

Boils; *to blight the swelling before matter forms; also externally, see page 126.*

Bright's disease; *chief remedy, and for the congestion, Ferric phosphate.*

Bronchitis, *second stage, when thick phlegm forms.*

Bruises, *if swelling, after the use of Ferric phosphate. Bubo, for swelling, if suppurative.*

Bunion; *also externally after Ferric phosphate; and if very hard, use Calcium fluoride.*

Catarrh; *phlegm white, not transparent; if not readily yielding, also Calcium fluoride.*

Carbuncles, *for the swelling; also as lotion on lint dressings alternately with Ferric phosphate if there is much inflammation.*

Chancre; *principal remedy throughout, 3rd trituration; and externally as a lotion.*

Chapped hands or lips *from cold; also applied as lotion.*

Cheek, *swollen; to control and reduce the swelling.*

Chilblains *on hands or feet or any part; also external use.*

Congestion *of any organ or part of the body; second stage, where there exists a white coated tongue, or expectoration of white mucus.*

Congestions; *in the second stage, there is interstitial exudation present, it causes swelling or enlargement of the parts.*

Cold *in the chest, with thick white or yellowish spit*

Cold *with a whitish or gray coated tongue.*

Cold *stuffy, in the head, with whitish-grey tongue.*

Cold *in the head, with white, non-transparent, or yellowish discharge.*

Colds, *any of the above not yielding to this remedy require Calcium fluoride.*

Condylomata, *warty excrescences ; internal and external use.*

Constipation; *light coloured stools, through want of bile from sluggish liver.*

Constipation; *which is accompanied by a white coated tongue; also when fat and pastry disagree.*

Cough, *in consumption, with thick white spit or white coated tongue.*

Cough, *loud, noisy, stomach cough, with greyish-white tongue.*

Cough, *with thick white or yellowish white phlegm.*

Cough, *stomachy, noisy, with protruded appearance of eyes, or itching at anus.*

Cough, *croupy, hard, with white coated tongue; use also Calc. fluoride.*

Cough, *with hoarseness, very persistent; Potass, sulph. in alternation.*

Croup, *the principal remedy for the membranous exudation; if fever is present, Ferric phos. Obstinate cases require Calcium fluoride.*

Crusta lactea, *milk crust, sore or scald head of children; principal remedy in alternation with Calcium sulphate.*

Cuts, *with swelling; as second remedy. See page 126.*

Cystitis, inflammation of the bladder, second stage; when swelling has set in (interstitial exudation), and discharge of thick white mucus.

Cystitis, chronic; the principal remedy.

Deafness, from swelling of the internal ear; primary remedy.

Deafness, (throat), from swelling of the Eustachian tubes.

Deafness, with swelling of the glands, or cracking noise on blowing the nose, or a white coated tongue; all these symptoms denote a disturbance of the molecules of this salt.

Diabetes, excess of urine which is sweet from the sugar contained in it; in alternation with the chief remedy, when the stomach and liver derangements show themselves by a gray or white coating on the tongue; pancreatic derangement; dry and light coloured stools from want of bile; pain in the kidneys. Avoid sugar and starchy food.

Diarrhœa, *if after fatty food, pastry, &c. Evacuations light coloured.*

Diarrhœa, *pale yellow, ochre or clay coloured stools.*

Diarrhœa, *in typhoid fever, stools like pale yellow ochre.*

Diarrhœa, *white, or slimy stools, generally with the characteristic white coating of tongue.*

Diphtheria; *the sole remedy in most cases in alternation with Ferric phosphate. Use gargle very frequently, 3d trituration, 4-5 grs, in tumbler of water. For prostration and adynamic condition, see Potassium phosphate.*

Discharges *of thick, white or yellowish slimy mucus, from the nose, ear, eyes, or any passage covered with a mucus membrane or lining.*

Dropsy, *arising from heart, liver, or kidney disease, when there are present prominent characteristic symptoms mentioned under ailments, page 145.*

Dropsy, *from obstruction of the bile ducts and enlargement of the liver, there is generally a white coating on the tongue.*

Dropsy, *from weakness of the heart; this remedy in alternation with Potassium phosphate.*

Dropsy, *with palpitation; also Potassium phosphate.*

Dropsy, *in which the liquid drawn off is whitish, or white mucus in sedi-*

ment of urine.

Dysentery; *purging with slimy bloody stools. In most cases this remedy with Ferric phosphate cures.*

Dyspepsia, *with a white or grayish coated tongue, pain or heavy feeling on the right side over the liver; especially if fatty food disagrees, or the eyes look large and projecting; if there is a dark appearance under the eyes give Potassium phosphate for this complication.*

Ear-ache, *with gray or white furred tongue.*

Ear-ache, *with swelling of the glands.*

Ear-ache, *with swelling of the throat, or cracking noise in the ear when swallowing.*

Eczema, *skin diseases arising after vaccination with bad vaccine lymph.*

Eczema, *resulting from suppressed or deranged uterine functions, generally with the characteristic white coating of tongue.*

Eczema, *skin affections, with oozing from the inflamed skin; in alternation with Ferric phosphate.*

Eczema, *if very obstinate, not yielding; use Calcium fluoride.*

Eczema, *with oozing of whitish opaque discharge and white coated tongue.*

Eczema, *skin affections, of vesicular form, or discharge of white secretions from the skin.*

Embolus; for that condition of blood which favours the formation of clots (fibrinous), which causes plugs; also Ferric phosphate for the circulatory disturbance.

Epilepsy, if occurring with, or after suppression of Eczema (eruptions).

Eruptions, pustules, pimples; also when discharging a whitish mattery substance.

Eruptions, on the skin (rash), if connected with stomach derangement, and there exists a white coated tongue.

Eruptions, accompanied with deranged menstrual period.

Erysipelas, vesicular (blistering); the chief remedy. For the fever, Ferric phosphate.

Erythema; after the use of Ferric phosphate, if there be any swelling or white coated tongue.

Exudations, after inflammation with effusion of lymph (effete albuminoid substance).

Exudations, fibrinous, in the interstitial connective-tissues, causing swelling or enlargement of these parts.

Excoriation, chafing of the skin, especially if inclined to scab, and if the coating on tongue is whitish.

Expectoration (spit) of white, opaque, slimy mucus (phlegm).

Eyes (sore), on the lid, specks of matter.

Eyes (sore), on the lids, yellow mattery crusts; chief remedy.

Eye, superficial fiat ulcer, arising from a vesicle.

Eye, opaque spots on the eye (Leucoma).

Eye, vesicle or blister on the eye.

Face-ache, with swelling of the gums or cheek.

Festers, gatherings in any part require this remedy for the swelling.

Gastritis, if caused from taking too hot drinks; this remedy at once.

Gastritis, with white coating of tongue, second stage.

Glandular swellings; chief remedy, but if very hard, Calcium fluoride.

Glands of the neck, swollen, require this remedy; also lotion on lint dressings externally.

Gonorrhœa; *principal remedy.*

Gumboil, *swelling before matter forms; in alternation with Ferric phosphate.*

Hœmorrhage, *clotted blood, black, thick or tough; also Calc. fluoride.*

Hœmorrhoids (bleeding piles), dark, thick blood; for the tumours or engorgement, Calcium fluoride.

Headache, with vomiting, hawking up of milk-white mucus.

Headache, sick, with white coated tongue, or vomiting of white phlegm.

Hip-joint disease, second stage, when swelling commences or is present.

Hoarseness, loss of voice from cold; if not yielding, use Potassium sulphate.

Hooping-cough, if there is a white-coated tongue, and thick white expectoration; for the whoop, Magnesium phosphate.

Indigestion, with white tongue, if caused by taking rich or fatty food.

Indigestion, with a sick feeling after taking fat; tongue generally furred gray or white.

Indigestion, vomiting of white opaque mucus.

Inflammations, all, in the second stage (exudations), in whatever organ or part of the body, require this salt, after or in alternation with or Ferric phosphate, the chief remedy.

Inflammation of skin, with subcutaneous swelling, *i.e.* second stage.

Inflammation of soft palate, catarrhal, with white spots or patches.

Injuries, from falls, blows, etc., with swelling of the parts; second remedy.

Intermittent fever, when the fur at the back of the tongue is of grayish or white appearance.

Intertrigo, (soreness, chafing of the skin of infants). See also Sodium chloride.

Jaundice, if the disease has been caused by a chill resulting in a catarrh of the duodenum, a white coated tongue; stools light coloured.

Lameness, rheumatic; with shiny, red swellings; also Calcium fluoride if not yielding altogether to this remedy.

Lameness, chronic, caused by rheumatism of the joints.

Liver, sluggish action of, sometimes pain in the right side, light yellow colour of the evacuations, denoting want of bile; use Potassium phosphate if the nerves are depressed.

Liver, sluggish action of, sluggish action of, generally accompanied by a white or grayish furred tongue, and constipation.

Lung disease, if the expectoration is whitish, thick, or yellowish-white and slimy. The tongue frequently coated with white fur at back.

Lungs, inflammation of, the second remedy; the tongue is generally white coated when this remedy is required.

Lupus; principal remedy. See Calcium phosphate.

Mastitis, "weed" (gathering breast); second remedy, to control the swelling. See also page 123.

Measles; for hearse cough, for all glandular swellings, and furred tongue, white or gray deposit; second remedy.

Measles; after effects of; diarrhœa, whitish, or light coloured loose stools, white tongue, deafness from swellings, etc.

Meningitis; as second remedy, will cut short the disease. For effusion, see page 51.

Menstruation, the monthly period delayed too late or suppressed, checked.

Menstruation, if too early or lasting too long. See also Potass, phos.

Menstruation, period, excessive, dark, clotted, or tough, black like tar.

Menstruation, period, bating too long, if other symptoms in this section detailed accompany it. See also Potassium phosphate.

Menstruation, courses or period suppressed. As above, or Potass, sulph.

Menstruation, too frequent.

Mumps; this remedy will cure alone, unless there be fever. With much saliva or swelling of testicles, Sodium chloride will also be required.

Morning sickness in pregnancy, with vomiting of white phlegm.

Orchitis; primary remedy, if from suppressed Gonorrhœa.

Palpitation, from excessive flow of blood to the heart; in hypertrophic conditions, also Ferric phosphate.

Pericarditis; this second remedy may complete the cure.

Peritonitis; this second remedy, following Ferric phosphate, generally completes the cure.

Pharyngitis, with swelling of the throat, grey or whitish exudation (spots or pustules); as second remedy.

Phlegm, mucus, discharge of, from any cavity lined with a mucous membrane, such as bronchi, throat, nasal cavity, vagina, etc., must be treated with this remedy when the secretion is white, yellowish, thick or slimy. It reduces the plastic exudation or waste matter there, accumulating for want of this cell-salt, thus restoring normal function.

Pimples on the face, neck, etc., caused by disturbed action of the follicular glands; if the skin is much inflamed, also Ferric phosphate.

Pleurisy; as second remedy, will complete the cure, after Ferric phos., as it is the healing salt for this group of ailments in second stage.

Pleurisy; second stage; after or in alternation with Ferric phosphate, for the plastic exudation; purely serous, Sodium chloride.

Proud flesh generally requires this remedy only, internally and externally.

Puerperal fever; this remedy alone may suffice for this disease, or in alternation with Ferric phosphate; for perverted brain function, Potassium phosphate,

Rheumatic fever, second stage, when exudation takes place, seen as swelling around the joints; this cell-salt will remove the swelling by restoring the non-functional cells of the excretory and absorbing-structures to normal action.

Rheumatic gouty pains, if movement makes them worse, and if there is a white or grey furred tongue.

Rheumatic pains, if there is swelling of the parts, and white or grey furred tongue.

Rheumatic pains, which are only felt during motion, or increased by it, if Ferric phosphate does not remove them altogether.

Rheumatism, chronic, with swelling, or when all movement causes pain; there is generally a grey or white fur at the back of the tongue.

Scabs, greenish, brown, or white, forming on pustules.

Scales, white, floury, proceeding from blisters.

Scales, on the scalp, white, without any increased watery secretions.

Scarlet fever; in mild cases it alone may suffice alternately with Ferric-phosphate for the febrile disturbance.

Scrofulous enlarged glands, enlarged abdomen with occasional diarrhœa, especially in the young.

Scurvy, hard infiltrations; the want of this salt is the cause of scurvy; it is readily cured by its use.

Secretions, white or yellowish slimy.

Shingles, with white coated tongue.

Sick headache, arising from a sluggish liver, when the tongue is furred at the back, looking grey or white.

Small-pox; the principal remedy; controls the formation of pustules.

Sores or ulcers, with whitish or dark grey tenacious crusts; when the parts are hard, swollen, and callous, Calcium fluoride.

Sprains; second remedy, if swelling remain.

Squinting, occasional, if caused by irritation from threadworms at anus.

Stomach, derangement of, with white or greyish coating at back of tongue.

Strumous conditions are benefitted by the use of this remedy and Calcium phosphate.

Swellings, plastic exudations, in general, are controlled by it.

Sgcosis (eruption on bearded part of face); primary remedy.

Syphilis, chronic stage.

Throat (sore), ulcerated, with patches of white or greyish colour; generally with the characteristic white tongue, which requires this remedy to heal these processes.

Toe-nail, ingrowing; also mechanical aid.

Tongue, coated greyish white, dryish or slimy, indicating that this cell-salt is required to restore the balance between the organic (albuminoid) and the inorganic substance (Potassium chloride).

Tongue, inflammation of, for the swelling.

Tonsils, inflammation of, when spotted, white or gray.

Tonsilitis (Quinsy), chronic or acute, with much swelling.

Toothache, with swelling of the gums.

Typhoid fever, for the grey or white deposit on the tongue; for the diarrhœa, with light yellow ochre coloured evacuations, and for abdominal tenderness and swelling.

Typhus, for constipation, stools light coloured; Ferric phos. for fever.

Ulcerations, all, when there is a swelling, or a dirty white surface and similar discharge. See also Calcium sulphate.

Ulceration of the os and cervix uteri, with the characteristic discharge of thick white or yellowish mild secretions (glandular or follicular) from the mucous membrane (alkaline).

Ulcers, with hard swelling; callous edges, Calcium fluoride.

Uterus, congestion of; hypertrophy, second stage, to heal or reduce this condition. See also Calcium fluoride.

Uvula, relaxed, when throat or tonsils are swollen.

Vomiting of blood, dark, clotted.

Vomiting hawking of thick white, or yellowish white, phlegm.

"Whites" (Leucorrhœa), discharge of milky white mucus, thick, sometimes yellowish, mild, non-irritating.

Wheezing, râle or rattling sound of air passing through thick tenacious mucus in the bronchi, difficult to cough up, hard cough.

Worms, small white threadworms, causing itching at anus; Ferric phosphate in alternation.

6.—Potassium Phosphate.

The Diseases forming this group must be healed or treated with *Potassium phosphate,* as they have their seat in some portion either of the nervous system, *i.e.* brain or nerves, or of the-muscles or blood corpuscles, of which this cell-salt is a constituent.

All Ailments, which arise from or denote a want of nerve power p hence nervous prostration, exhaustion, nervous rigors; and also-all those affections in which the brain, and consequently the mind, shows want of vigour. Alternation of this remedy may often be required whenever symptoms of exhaustion or want of power in any of the nerves occur, nervousness; or in those cases where there is rapid decomposition of the blood, causing foul putrid conditions, mortification, and septic conditions.

Ague, for heavy exhausting sweats.

Amenorrhœa, *retention or delay of the monthly flow, with depression of spirits, lassitude, and general nervous debility.*

Anœmia, *poverty of blood, from continuous influences, depressing; the mind, or rather the nerves.*

Anœmia, cerebral; anæmic morbid conditions of the brain, causing: undue nervousness.

Anxiety, nervous dread without special cause, gloomy moods, fancies, taking dark views of things, dark forebodings.

Asthma; in often repeated, large doses, this is the chief remedy for the depressed condition of the nervous system, and the breathing.

Asthma; bronchial, treatment same as above; for expectoration, see; pages 70-71.

Atrophy, wasting disease, when putrid-smelling stools set in.

Breath, offensive, fœtid; tongue coated like brownish liquid mustard.

Bladder, paralysis of sphincter muscle, causing inability of retaining the urine, generally of old people.

Bleeding of the gums, predisposition to.

Blood, loss of, if dark, blackish, thin, not coagulating.

Brain-fag, from over-work, with loss of appetite, stupor, depressed spirits, irritability or great impatience, loss of memory, or sleeplessness.

Bright's disease (of the kidneys), for the depressed condition of the nerves, showing itself in sleeplessness, irritability, weary feeling.

Cancer, encephaloid, medullary, soft (brain-like convolutions), chiefly occurring in the young. This was hitherto considered more serious and less amenable to treatment than the hard.

Catamenia, premature and profuse in nervous subjects.

Chancre, phagadænic.

Chattering of the teeth, nervous, not from cold.

Cholera, first stage; diarrhœa, when the stools have the appearance of rice water.

Collapse, with livid, bluish countenance, and low pulse.

Concussion of brain; give this remedy in alternation with Ferric phos.

Croup, if treatment is delayed till last stage; for extreme weakness, pale or livid countenance, in alternation with Potass, chloride.

Crying or screaming in children, from undue sensitiveness.

Cystitis, inflammation of the bladder; in asthenic condition, with prostration.

Deafness, from want of nervous perception, deadening of the auditory nerve.

Deafness, weakness, exhaustion of the auditory nerve.

Diabetes; to establish normal function of the medulla oblongata and pneumogastric nerve, which latter acts on the digestion or stomach, and on the lungs. The symptom for which this remedy must be given is nervous weakness; in Diabetes melitus the urine is sweet, containing sugar; breath peculiar, with haylike odour, deranged kidneys, thirst, emaciation, and often voracious hunger, all consequent on liver derangement.

Debility, general, with nervousness and irritability.

Delirium tremens, the horrors of drunkards; fear, sleeplessness, restlessness and suspiciousness, rambling talk, endeavours to grasp or avoid visionary images. Sodium chloride must be given alternately for the purpose of restoring the normal consistency of brain substance, which in this disease is disturbed.

Depression of spirits and lassitude.

Diarrhœa, *foul; also, if accompanying any other disease, to heal the conditions causing putrid evacuations.*

Diarrhœa, *with heavy odour, occasioned by fright and other causes, depressing and exhausting the nerves.*

Diphtheria, *after effects of; weakness of sight, or paralysis in any part.*

Diphtheria, *the well-marked gangrenous condition.*

Diphtheria, *for exhausted prostrate conditions at any stage.*

Dispiritedness, *feeling of faintness.*

Dread *of noise, over sensitiveness to noise or light.*

Dysentery, when the stool consists of blood only, and the patient becomes delirious (brainish), abdomen swollen; or if the stools have a putrid odour, this remedy must be given.

Dysentery, with putrid, very offensive stools.

Ears, noises in the, from nervous exhaustion.

Eczema, if nervous irritation and over sensitiveness accompany it; this salt may be taken as an intercurrent remedy.

Encephaloma, soft cancer. (Brain-like convolutions).

Epilepsy, with pallor, sunken countenance, coldness and palpitation after the fit.

Epileptic fits, "falling sickness," from abnormal condition of some of the nerve cells. If accompanied by coldness of the limbs, great pallor, and shrunken appearance of the face; and also, if after the fit there is violent palpitation of the heart, give this remedy.

Epistaxis, bleeding of the nose, and predisposition to, from weakness.

Evacuations, putrid, very offensive smell.

Excessive hungry feeling, soon after taking food, caused by nervous depression or weakness.

Exhaustion from any cause, which has lowered the nervous system.

Eyes, starry appearance of the, when connected with nervous affections, or as a symptom during the course of a disease.

Eyesight, weak, from an exhausted condition of the optic nerve.

Face-ache, neuralgia, with great exhaustion after the attack.

Face, livid and sunken, with hollow eyes.

Fainting, from weak action of the heart

Faintness, feeling of, in nervous people.

Faintness, feeling of, or dizziness without gastric derangement.

Faintness, from weak action of the heart.

Flatulence, with distress about the heart.

Fits, from fright, with pallid or livid countenance,

Gangrenous conditions, mortification in the first stage; to heal those pathological conditions which give rise to it.

Gastritis (inflammation of stomach), if it comes too late under treatment, with asthenic conditions.

Hay-Asthma, for the depression and asthmatic breathing; in alternation with Sodium chloride.

Headache, nervous, sensitiveness to noise, irritability, confusion.

Headache, which is relieved by motion.

Headache, of students and those worn out by fatigue, when no gastric symptoms are felt, but the tongue is sometimes found to be coated brownish yellow, like stale mustard.

Head, pains and weight at the back of the, with feeling of weariness and exhaustion; to be taken after Ferric phosphate.

Heart complaint, functional, intermittent, with palpitation.

Heart, intermittent action of the, with morbid nervous sensitiveness.

Heart, intermittent action of the, effects of violent emotions, grief or care.

Hœmorrhage, **blood not coagulating, thin, blackish or light red. See also** **Sodium chloride.**

Hoarseness, **with exhausted feeling from over-exertion of voice, and with** **nervous depression; also recent paralysis of vocal chords.**

Hooping-cough, **in the highly nervous, or with great exhaustion.**

Home sickness, **morbid activity of memory, haunted by visions of the past,** **and longing after them.**

Hypochondriasis —melancholy: when accompanied by liver complications, see Sodium sulphate, or Potassium chloride.

Hysteria in females, nervous attacks, from sudden or intense emotion, or from smothering passion, in the highly nervous and excitable; also a feeling as of a ball rising in the throat.

Hysterical fits of laughter and crying.

Incontinence of urine from paralysis of the sphincter of the bladder.

Indigestion, with great nervous depression.

Intermittent fever, fœtid debilitating profuse perspiration.

Infantile paralysis, recent, and if connected with teething, give also Calcium phosphate.

Irritability, undue, after exhausting diarrhœa or long-continued use of purgatives.

Insanity, mania or other mental derangement; all arising from exhausted or depressed condition of some brain or nerve cells, showing itself in perverted function of the brain.

Lameness, recent, paralytic, from exhaustion of the nerves, with stiffness after rest, yielding however to gentle exercise.

Lameness, rheumatic, rigidity of the muscles, the pain alleviated by gentle exercise.

Labour pains, if feeble and ineffectual; also against spurious labour pains.

Mastitis, if the pus is brownish, dirty-looking, with heavy odour, to heal the adynamic condition. See also page 126 for external uses.

Melancholia and other similar ailments, which arise from deranged mental function, caused by over-strain of the mind, or from exhausting drainings affecting the nerve centres of the spinal cord.

Memory, bad or loss of; Calcium phos. as an intercurrent remedy.

Menstrual colic, in lachrymose, over-sensitive, irritable, pale females.

Menstruation, too late, in pale, irritable, sensitive, lachrymose females; to heal the pathological conditions which give rise to this.

Menstruation, too scanty, in similar constitutions.

Menstruation, too profuse discharge, with heavy odour, dark red, or blackish red, thin, and not coagulating.

Nervous affections, when occurring without reasonable causes, such as impatience, irritability, dwelling upon grievances, merriment becoming oppressive, shedding tears about trifles, making " mountains out of mole hills."

Nervousness in its various manifestions requires this salt.

Night terrors, in children awakening in a great fright and screaming.

Noises in the head on falling asleep, feeling as if a rocket had passed through the head.

Noma, water canker.

Neuralgic pains, better with gentle exercise, worse on rising.

Œdema pulmonarium, *with livid countenance.*

Pains, *bodily, disposition to feel too acutely.*

Pains, *laming, which are better with gentle exercise, worse on first-rising up, or through exertion; to heal the abnormal condition of nerve cells.*

Palpitation, *from nervous causes.*

Palpitation, *on ascending, with shortness of breath.*

Palpitation, *with nervousness, anxiety.*

Palpitation, *with sleeplessness.*

Paralysis, *facial, loss of power in the muscles of the face, causing contortions or an involuntary twist of the mouth.*

Paralysis, *shock of, with morbid sensibility, or a bruised and painful feeling in the part affected, or rigidity of the paralysed limbs. This remedy must be given to arrest its progress, and to prevent its recurrence.*

Paralysis, *atrophic, in which the vital powers are reduced.*

Paralysis, *creeping, in which the progress of the disease is slow, and there is a tendency to wasting, with loss of the sense of touch, &c.*

Perspirations, *excessive, exhausting, with heavy odour.*

Perspirations, *during meals, with a feeling of weakness at the pit of the stomach.*

Puerpural *"childbed" fever, when absurd notions or mania sets in.*

Pulse, intermittent, *irregular, from exhausting causes.*

Pulse, intermittent, *below the normal standard from enfeebled nervous system.*

Purpura, *"land scurvy," to heal the adynamic processes.*

Restlessness and irritability, *from nervous causes.*

Rickets, *atrophy, with putrid evacuations.*

Rheumatism, *acute and chronic, with pains disappearing on moving about, severe in the morning after, rest, and on first rising from sitting position.*

Scarlet fever; *putrid condition of throat, also for all typhoid symptoms.*

Sciatica, *rheumatic or neuralgic affection of the sciatic nerve which extends down the back of the thigh to the knee, when moving gives relief; also Ferric phos. if symptoms of heat or fever arise.*

Septic bleedings, *blood prutrid.*

Sensitiveness, *too keen, from want of nerve.*

Sighing and depression, *with inclination to look at the "dark side" of things.*

Sighing and depression, or moaning, *also when occurring during sleep.*

Shortness of breath, *asthmatic.*

Shortness of breath, *when going up a stair.*

Shortness of breath, *with any symptom showing want of nerve power or exhaustion.*

Shyness, *excessive blushing, from undue sensitiveness of the nerves.*

Sleeplessness, *after worry or excitement, showing the source of such condition to be a want of this cell salt in the nerves.*

Sleeplessness, *simple wakefulness.*

Sleeplessness, *from nervous causes; to heal those nerve cells, which do not act normally.*

Sluggish circulation, *in sensitive nervous subjects; to strengthen the heart's action.*

Smallpox, *with putrid condition and exhaustion.*

Softening of the brain, *early stage; if connected with hydrocephalus or water on the brain, then give also Calcium phosphate.*

Softening of the brain, *as the result of inflammation: Ferric phosphate must also be given. This kind of softening is sometimes very insiduous in its approach.*

Speech, *slow and becoming inarticulate, frequently connected with creeping paralysis.*

Spinal cord, softening of, *idiopathic, with gradual deadening of the nerves. This remedy must be given to arrest its progress.*

Starting *on being touched, or at sudden noises.*

Stomatitis (ulcers of the mouth) with foetid offensive breath.

Suppurations, dirty foul ichorous matter, with offensive odour.

Temperature, high, of the body in disease; to strengthen those nerves which control the function of the blood vessels.

Tongue, coated, like stale brownish liquid mustard, offensive breath.

Tongue, coated, excessively dry in the morning, feeling as if it would cleave to the roof of the mouth.

Toothache, of highly nervous, delicate, or pale, irritable sensitive persons.

Toothache, with easily bleeding gums.

Typhoid states, or all malignant conditions, when occurring during the course of a disease.

Vertigo, giddiness from nervous exhaustion and weakness, and not from gastric derangement.

Weakness of sight from exhaustion; to heal or restore nervous vigour.

Weakness of sight loss of perceptive power in the optic nerve.

Weakness of sight if after diphtheria; see also Silica.

Whining and fretful disposition in children and adults,

Yawning, excessive, unnatural, which arises from nervous causes, if accompanied with a sensation of emptiness of the stomach although food has been partaken of.

7.—Potassium Sulphate.

The Diseases forming this group must be healed or treated with **Potassium Sulphate** A want of this constituent cell-salt causes yellow slimy deposit on the tongue, sticky, thin, decidedly yellow discharges or secretions of watery matter.

All Ailments which become worse in the evening, or in a warm room, and grow better in a cool or open atmosphere. Ailments accompanied with desquamation, peeling of the skin, or with itching pimples arising singly on the skin. Also all which are caused by sudden retrocession of eruptions (rash).

Bronchitis, if the mucus is distinctly yellow and slimy, thin, or watery mattery and profuse.

Cancer, epithelial. See Epithelioma.

Catarrh, chronic, of the stomach; when there is a yellow slimy coated tongue. If an acute disease sets in, the coating of the tongue may not change, therefore look for other characteristic symptoms in selecting the remedy for the new disease.

Catarrhs, colds, with yellow slimy secretions or expectorations of watery matter.

Catarrh, if of the stomach, with a yellow slimy coated tongue.

Cold, in the head, with decidedly yellow slimy discharge; note also tongue.

Dandriff, yellow scales on the scalp.

Deafness, from swelling of tympanic cavity, or watery mattery discharge from the ear, or if the tongue has a yellow slimy coating.

Deafness, throat, with catarrh, causing swelling of eustachian tubes, and inner ear with symptoms as above.

Deafness, when worse in a warm room; with yellow slimy coated tongue.

Diarrhœa, *yellow, slimy, or watery mattery stools; note also coating of tongue.*

Dryness of skin, *with scaling, from suppressed skin disease.*

Dyspepsia, *indigestion, with decidedly yellow slimy coated tongue.*

Ears, *with secretion of thin yellow sticky fluid after inflammation. See also page 126.*

Eczema, *skin affections; when the characteristic abnormal conditions present are denoting a disturbed function of the cells containing this salt, there will be a casting out of effete matter, a discharge decidedly yellow, slimy, sometimes sticky, or watery mattery.*

Eczema, *skin affections, when suddenly suppressed, if any characteristic symptoms are present for which this remedy is given.*

Effusions, *watery mattery.*

Epithelioma, *cancer on the skin near a mucous lining, with discharge of thin yellow sticky or watery mattery secretions. Ext. use, p. 126.*

Eruptions, *when suddenly receding either through a chill, or from other causes.*

Eyelids, *with thin, yellow crusts.*

Eyes, discharge from; *yellow slimy or sticky watery matter.*

Face-ache, *aggravated in the warm room and in the evening; improved in cool or open air.*

Headache, *which grows worse in the warm room and in the evening, and is better in cool or open air.*

Hoarseness, *from cold. If not removed by Potassium chloride.*

Hooping-cough; *for decidedly yellow slimy expectoration; for the whoop, Magnesium phosphate.*

Indigestion, *with sensation of pressure as of a load, and fulness at the pit of the stomach. See Dyspepsia.*

Inflammations, with yellow, slimy secretions or excessive serous secretions if Potassium chlor. does not absorb these completely.

Leucorrhœa, "Whites," discharge of decidedly yellow slimy or watery mattery secretions.

Lungs, inflammation of, with wheezing; if yellow loose rattling phlegm be coughed up with difficulty, or consists of watery matter.

Menstruation, too late and too scanty, with a feeling of weight and fulness in abdomen.

Nails, for diseased condition of, shown in interrupted growth. See also Silica.

Nettle-rash, with or without yellow slimy tongue, generally caused by indigestion. See also Sodium chloride,

Pains in the back, nape of the neck, or in the limbs, if periodically worse in the evening, or in a warm room, and if decidedly better in a cool or open atmosphere, or in the open air.

Piles, internal and external, may require this remedy in alternation with Calcium fluoride the chief remedy, only if the tongue is coated yellow slimy, and discharges or secretions of this characteristic type are present.

Rash, of measles or other erruptive ferbile diseases, when suppressed or suddenly receding, with harsh and dry skin. This remedy will assist the returning of the rash.

Rheumatic fever, when articular pains are shifting, wandering.

Rheumatic headaches, always beginning in the evening, and in a warm room.

Rheumatic pains in the joints, shifting, wandering, chronic or acute.

Rheumatism, acute, articular, when of a shifting nature; neuralgia pains require Magnesium phosphate.

Rheumatism, chronic of the joints, with characteristic symptoms pointing to this remedy.

Scarlet fever, desquamation, *i.e.,* skin peeling off, the infectious stages of scarlet fever, etc.; this salt assists desquamation, and formation of new healthy skin.

Skin, sores on, with yellow, sticky secretions on limited portions, or discharges of thin watery matter, sometimes with peeling of the surrounding skin.

Smallpox, in; to promote the formation of new healthy skin, and the falling off of the crusts.

Tongue, coating of, yellow, slimy, sometimes with whitish edge.

Toothache, aggravated in the warm room and in the evening, but better in the cool, open air.

8.—Magnesium phosphate.

The Diseases forming this group must be healed or treated with ***Magnesium*** *phosphate,* as these diseases have their seat either in the muscle or nerve cells. It is the true anti-spasmodic remedy.

All Ailments, which are of a darting, crampy, spasmodic nature, often accompanied with a feeling of constriction and pressure, and when warmth is soothing or agreeable. The remedy may be taken in hot liquids.

Angina pectoris, breast pang; for the neuralgic spasms. The remedy had best be given in hot water.

Back, neuralgic pains in, very acute, darting, boring, shifting about, and remittent.

Bowels and Stomach, gnawing pains in, with flatulent distension, slight short belching of gas (wind) giving no relief.

Choleraic cramps.

Chorea, St. Vitus' dance, involuntary movements and contortions of the limbs, with mute appealing look for sympathy.

Chromatopsia, spasmodic vision of sparks or of rainbow colours.

Colic, flatulent, of children, with drawing up of legs.

Colic, forcing the patient to bend double, pain eased by friction, warmth, and eructations.

Colic, in umbilical region, forcing the patient to bend forward.

Colic, remittent, gripes, crampy pain.

Constriction of chest and throat, with spasmodic, dry, tickling cough.

Convulsive twitching of the corners of the mouth.

Convulsions, with stiffness of the limbs or of the body, thumbs drawn in, fingers clenched; if convulsions occur in children, give Calcium phosphate alternately.

Cough, spasmodic, coming in fits, paroxysms.

Cough, true spasmodic.

Cramp, of the legs, or indeed in any part of the body; if there is decided numbness, use also Calcium phosphate.

Cramp, spasm of throat, closing of the larynx.

Diplopia, seeing double, an affection of the eye.

Dysentery, with crampy pain, eased by bending double, by warmth, or friction.

Dysentery, with crampy stomach-ache, eased by warmth.

Epigastric pains at pit of stomach, nipping, griping, with short belching of wind giving no relief.

Epigastric pains spasms, cramp in the stomach, with clean tongue, crampy pain as if a band were tightly laced or drawn round the body.

Epileptic fits, spasm, stiffness of the limbs, clenched fists or teeth; Calcium phosphate may have to be alternated.

Epilepsy, from local irritation of the nerves, when an over excited not depressed condition of the nerves exists; sometimes the result of vicious habits, which must be restrained.

Epilepsy, for the muscular contractions, the twitchings and spasms, a course of this remedy may be taken as a tonic,

Face-ache (neuralgic, rheumatic), stinging, shooting like lightning, darting about; and remittent.

Glottis, spasm of the, causing contraction of the opening of the windpipe, a struggle for breath, and a feeling of suffocation, sometimes with stiffness of the limbs.

Gravel, windy pain.

Headaches, very excruciating, with tendency to spasmodic symptoms.

Headaches, (neuralgic, rheumatic), shooting or stinging, shifting and intermittent.

Hooping cough, beginning as a common cold, Ferric phosphate as first remedy, but for the convulsive fits of nervous cough ending in a whoop, give Magnesium phosphate.

Intermittent fever, with cramp of the calves.

Labour pain, spasmodic, with cramp in legs.

Labour pain, excessive, crampy expulsive efforts.

Laryngismus stridulus, cramp or spasm of the larynx (windpipe), also called "child-crowing."

Limbs, pains in (neuralgic, rheumatic), very vivid, darting about, shifting, and remittent.

Menstrual colic; the chief remedy in ordinary cases.

Nape of neck, pains in, very sharp, shooting, boring, shifting, and remittent

Neuralgia, intercostal (between the ribs), of a drawing, constrictive kind; spasms from cold.

Neuralgia in the head, pains darting and very sharp. If inflammatory or congestive, the pain is deep-seated and localised, and must be treated with Ferric phosphate alternately.

Ovarian neuralgia, if the pain is shooting, and darting like lightning; if only burning and stitching, use Ferric phosphate.

Pains, neuralgic, in any part, when darting or shooting along the nerve.

Pains, spasmodic, in the stomach or bowels, griping, cutting, drawing, so as to bend the body double, increased on the slightest muscular movement.

Palsy, involuntary shaking and trembling of the hands or limbs, or of the head; an affection of muscles and nerves.

Puerpural convulsions.

Retention of urine, inability to pass water from spasmodic constriction after use of catheter, a sensation as if the muscles did not contract; for fever, if present, Ferric phosphate.

Shaking of the hands, trembling, even when caused by alcoholism.

Shaking, spasmodic trembling, from want of nervous control of the muscles in any part of the body.

Sparks before the eyes —photopsia.

Spasmodic affections of the eyelids (twitching).

Spasmodic cough at night, with difficulty of lying down.

Spasmodic pains and affections of almost any kind.

Spasm of the throat, on attempting to swallow liquids.

Squinting, spasmodic, in children; give also Calcium phosphate.

St. Vitus' dance; chief remedy.

Stammering, spasmodic; to remove the spasmodic action of the muscles; Potassium phosphate for nervousness. Begin your speech with the teeth clenched.

Strabismus, spasmodic squinting. When in children, give Calcium phosphate alternately.

Stricture, spasmodic of the bladder.

Teething, convulsions, cramps, without fever; in alternation with Calcium phosphate.

Tetanus (lockjaw).

Toothache, if hot liquids ease the pain; bat if the application of cold ease the pain, it is inflammatory, and most be treated with Ferric phosphate. Seepage 125.

Toothache, (neuralgic, rheumatic), very intense and shooting, eased by warmth.

Tonic spasms.

Trembling, involuntary shaking of the hands and limbs.

Yawning, with excessive spasmodic straining of the lower jaw.

9.—Sodium Chloride.

The Diseases forming this group must be healed or treated with **Sodium Chloride;** they arise from a disturbed balance of the molecules of this salt, which is a constituent of all solids and fluids of the body, and its presence regulates the proper degree of moisture of solids and the watery consistency of fluids.

All Ailments, of any kind, when the salivary glands secrete too much saliva. The tongue has a clear slimy appearance, or small bubbles of frothy saliva extend along its sides; and when there exists an involuntary watery discharge or flow of tears, or when there are increased watery secretions, discharges from any of the mucous membranes, with co-existing want of activity in some other portion of the mucous linings.

Adynamic conditions, with drowsiness, watery vomiting, etc.

Aphthœ, *thrush, with flow of saliva.*

Asthma, *with profuse frothy mucus; in alternation with Potas. phos.*

Bronchitis, *acute inflammation of the windpipe, with frothy and clear starchy phlegm, loose and rattling, and sometimes coughed up with difficulty.*

Bronchitis, *chronic, bronchial catarrh, with any of the above symptoms.*

Catarrhs, *chronic, of bloodless patients, the mucus has sometimes a salty taste.*

Chilliness, *and almost habitual feeling of coldness in the back, with characteristic appearance of tongue, etc.*

Chlorotic conditions, *like "greensickness," if any of the above symptoms are present.*

Constipation, *chronic: the concurrent symptoms must decide this choice.*

Constipation, *with morbid secretions of the mucous membrane, frothy saliva, etc.*

Coryza (cold in head), with watery, clear, slimy or starchy discharge.

Cough, in consumption, chronic, with excess of watery secretions.

Dandruff, white scales on scalp, with excess of watery secretions from the mouth, nose, or eyes.

Deafness, from swelling of the tympanic cavity, with watery condition of the tongue as above, or watery secretions.

Delirium, occurring at any time, with starting of the body, picking at the bed clothes, 'wandering delirium, and muttering, with frothy or very dry tongue; fever; requires also Ferric phosphate.

Diarrhœa, *with transparent, glassy, slimy stools.*

Diphtheria, *if face be puffy and pale, with flow of watery fluid, and dryness of tongue; drowsiness; or watery stools.*

Dropsy, *after scarlatina, with characteristic symptoms calling for the use of this remedy.*

Drowsiness, *excessive and unnatural stupor, with saliva dribbling from the mouth in sleep.*

Eczema, *white, scaly. See external application, p. 126.*

Effusions, serous (of a colourless fluid); note also if other symptoms characteristic of a disturbed condition of this cell salt are present.

Eruptions of small vesicles or blisters with colourless watery fluid, forming into scabs or crusts, which fall off and readily form again.

Eyes, discharge of clear mucus from, or flow of tears with obstruction of the tear duct. For inflammatory condition use Ferric phos.

Eyes, (neuralgic) pains, periodically appearing, with flow of tears.

Eyes, affection of, with secretion of water, sensitiveness to light, and flow of tears causing scalded skin or eruption of small vesicles.

Face-ache, with constipation; tongue showing a clear mucous slime, and little frothy bubbles at its edge.

Face-ache, with vomiting of clear phlegm or water.

Fingers, blistering festers on, containing watery bloody fluid, often caused! by arsenical wall papers.

Glands, salivary, chronic inflammation of, with corresponding symptoms, excess of saliva, etc.

Glands, lymphatic; chronic swelling, if with corresponding watery symptoms.

Gonorrhœa, *if with the characteristic secretions for which this salt has to be given.*

Hay-fever, *for the watery discharge from the eyes and nose; some of the lotion may also be sniffed up into the nostrils; for the fever,. Ferric phosphate; the asthmatic trouble, Potassium phosphate.*

Headache, *dull heavy, with profusion of tears, and drowsiness.*

Headaches, *with constipation, from torpor and dryness of a portion of the internal mucous membrane; when tongue covered with clear slimy mucus, frothy edges, or much saliva.*

Headaches, *with vomiting of transparent phlegm or water.*

Hœmorrhage, *bleeding; blood pale red, thin, watery, not coagulating.*

Herpatic eruptions, *occurring alone or during the course of a disease.*

Herpes *or letter, an inflammation of the skin accompanied by small blebs, blisters, or watery vesicles.*

Herpes-zoster, *as second remedy.*

Hooping-cough, *if the mucus is frothy, clear, and stringy.*

Housemaid's knee, for enlargement of bursæ, this cell salt is the chief remedy.

Hydrocele, when the secretions are watery.

Influenza, with watery, frothy expectoration, running at the nose, great sleepiness. For the fever and bruised feeling in the back, the limbs, or the bones, give Ferr. phos. alternately. These salts when used early, will often prevent the development of the disease.

Intermittent fever, with vomiting of water, or clear slimy glairy mucus, like white of egg.

Intertrigo, soreness of skin of children, with watery symptoms.

Jaundice, with any of the symptoms present, peculiar to this group of ailments.

Kidney (Bright's disease) with characteristic symptoms calling for the use of the above remedy.

Knee, chronic swelling of, particularly if scrofulous.

Leucorrhœa, ("Whites") a watery, scalding, irritating discharge between the periods.

Lethargic state, with jerking or starting of the limbs, excessive drowsiness, stupor, eyes half open.

Looseness of the bowels, with watery stools; avoid excessive use of salt.

Lungs, inflammation of, if there is much loose rattling phlegm, clear and frothy, and coughed up with difficulty, and when it has not been absorbed by the use of Potassium chloride.

Measles, if there is an excessive secretion of tears or saliva; as an intercurrent remedy.

Morning sickness, with vomiting of watery frothy phlegm.

Mumps, with much salivation.

Nettle-rash, with accompanying watery symptoms.

Neuralgia, periodic, with great flow of saliva or tears.

Œdema of lungs, *acute; serous, frothy secretions.*

Orchitis, after suppression of gonorrhœa, if with characteristic secretions.

Orchitis, arising after suppression of mumps.

Pemphigus, blisters starting up on burning spots, with clear watery contents; also external applications.

Pleurisy, when during and after its course serous effusion has taken place.

Polyuria, in Diabetes mellitus, if the symptoms correspond.

Rheumatic fever, after the second remedy, and where the characteristic symptoms of this group indicate it.

Rheumatic gouty pain, if symptoms of tongue, or watery discharges, or secretions, etc., correspond.

Rheumatism of the joints, chronic; if tongue or other symptoms correspond, and if joints crack.

Rupia, blisters, not pustular eruptions.

Salivation, excess of saliva, whether existing alone or accompanying any other disease.

Scarlet fever, with drowsiness, twitchings, dryness of tongue, or vomiting of watery fluids.

Scales on the scalp, see Dandruff.

Secretions, discharges, if frothy, clear, slimy.

Secretions, if clear, like white of egg, or stringy.

Secretions, if clear, like boiled starch.

Secretions, on the skin, watery, not sticky, with other corresponding symptoms; if not yielding to this, use Sodium sulphate.

Shingles, with the characteristic symptoms of this group of ailments.

Sick headache, with vomiting or coughing up of clear water or starchlike mucus.

Skin, chafing of, in infants; generally with watery symptoms.

Sleepiness, sleep unrefreshing, feeling tired in the morning on awaking, constant and excessive inclination to sleep, when accompanied with one or other of above characteristic symptoms. See also Sodium sulphate.

Small-pox, with salivary flow, confluence of pustules, and drowsiness.

Stings of insects. Apply the lotion externally as soon as possible; the remedy may also be taken internally.

Stomach-ache, with much water (saliva) gathering in the mouth; if not curative, the tongue must be examined for symptoms calling for Potassium sulphate.

Sunstroke The pathological conditions of this affection show the fluidity of the blood deficient, from sudden abstraction of moisture at the nape of the neck. Sodium chloride is the necessary remedy in these conditions.

Sycosis (affection of the bearded part of face), if the (watery) symptoms correspond.

Teething, with much dribbling and flow of saliva, caused by disturbed condition of this cell-salt, which, if normally acting, regulates such secretions.

Throat enlargement, cystic, goitrous; also Calcium fluoride.

Throat enlargement, inflammation of the mucous lining, with transparent frothy mucus, covering the tonsils.

Tongue, appearance of, clear, slimy, and when small bubbles of frothy saliva cover the sides.

Toothache, with involuntary flow of tears.

Toothache, with great flow of saliva.

Typhoid conditions, during the course of any fever, twitchings, with great drowsiness, dryness of tongue, watery vomiting.

Uvula, relaxed, if there is much saliva. See also Calcium fluoride.

Vomiting of transparent, tough, stringy mucus.

Vomiting of watery fluids (not acid).

"Whites"—Leucorrhoea, watery, smarting or clear starchy-like discharges, after or between the periods.

10.—Sodium Phosphate.

The Diseases or pathological conditions forming this group must be-healed or treated with **Sodium phosphate;** they arise mainly from excess of lactic acid, composed of carbonic acid and water, the product of sugar.

All Ailments, in which there are symptoms of acidity; deposit on the-tongue of a thin moist, yellow coating (gold-coloured) like honey, sometimes covering the tongue as if with moist brown sugar, or the-soft palate has a yellowish creamy look.

Acidity, sour risings.

Appetite, loss of, indigestion felt slightly; on rising in the morning tongue has a thin moist deposit at the back, as if raw brown sugar bad just been partaken of.

Ague or intermittent fever, tongue with moist coating, yellow with a. golden tinge and moist.

Colic, of children, with symptoms of acidity, such as green, sour-smelling stools, etc,

Diabetes mellitus, if symptoms of acidity predominate, or if there is any ulceration of the mucous membrane or tongue.

Diarrhœa, *caused by excess of acidity, stools sour smelling.*

Diseases, *where the throat is implicated, and the tonsils are coated with a deposit, having a yellow or gold-coloured tinge.*

Ears, sore; *the outer part of the ear about the seam, with slight thin cream like scabbing, and the deposit on the tongue looks as if raw brown sugar had been eaten.*

Ears, sore; *one ear red, hot, and frequently itchy, accompanied by gastric derangement and acidity.*

Eyes, *discharge of yellow creamy matter.*

Eyes, inflammation of, *conjunctivitis, discharge of yellow creamy matter, the lids glued together in the mornings; note also conditions of tongue, and back of palate.*

Flatulence, *with sour risings.*

Gastric derangements, *with predominating symptoms of acidity.*

Headache, *from taking thick sour milk.*

Heartburn, *if with symptoms of acidity; note the tongue.*

Indigestion, *with characteristic tongue indicating this remedy, or acidity.*

Intermittent fever, *with vomiting of acid, sour masses.*

Morning sickness, *with vomiting of sour masses or fluids.*

Nausea, *sickness, with sour risings.*

Pains, *various, if the tongue, tonsils, or the palate has a golden-tinged deposit, like half-dried cream, or honey coloured.*

Perspirations, *acid, excessively sour smelling.*

Scabs, *if golden yellow, like honey.*

Secretions, *discharges of slime or mucus, if green and acid.*

Secretions, *discharges of matter, if green, and if acidity exist.*

Sore patches on skin, *red, with yellow gold-coloured coating on tongue.*

Sores, *with yellow creamy discharge. This effete organic substance is thrown out for want of Sodium phosphate.*

Squinting, *occasionally, if caused by intestinal irritation from worms; there are often acid risings, or symptoms peculiar to this group of ailments.*

Throat, sore, raw feeling with a moist deposit on the tongue in the morning on rising, looking yellow as if raw (brown) sugar had just been partaken of. For feverishness, Ferric phosphate.

Tongue, coating at the back, golden yellow, creamy moist, not slimy. When Sodium phosphate is medicinally required, and the molecular motion of its particles in any of the cells is disturbed, the tongue has generally its characteristic appearance. On rising in the morning, the deposit on back of tongue has a moist, yellow look, with a gold-like tinge, as if raw (brown) sugar had just been par-taken of.

Ulcers, ulceration of the stomach.

Ulceration of the bowels; Ferric phos. may also be required alternately.

Vomiting of acid (sour) masses.

Vomiting by children of curdled masses and acid fluids.

Water-brash, with acidity.

Worms, intestinal, long, with characteristic symptoms of the tongue, or of acidity.

11.— Sodium Sulphate.

The Diseases forming this group must be healed or treated with *Sodium sulphate* They arise from a disturbance in the molecular motion of this salt in the tissues, causing non-elimination of such water from the tissues as is produced by oxidation of organic substances.

All Ailments, in which there is accumulation of water in the areolar tissues, causing watery secretions on the skin, or greenish exudations from the mucous membranes, including those marked by excessive secretion of bile and derangement of the liver; and those characterized by a dirty greenish-grey or greenish-brown coating of the tongue.

Biliousness, when there really is excess of bile, bitter taste in the mouth, greenish-brown or greenish-grey tongue, or greenish diarrhœa, dark bilious stools. White or grey coated tongue requires Potassium chloride, and marks the *want* of bile.

Bilious colic, with bitter taste in the mouth, and grayish or brownish green coating at the root of the tongue.

Bilious colic, derangement, if too much bile is secreted, there is bitter taste in the mouth in the morning, with or without characteristic tongue; but frequently so-called bilious derangements are liver derangements, arising from want of bile, and require Potassium chloride.

Bilious colic, fever, remittent. See intermittent fever.

Bilious colic, fever, with bitter taste in mouth, characteristic tongue; also Ferric phosphate for feverishness.

Bowels, heat in the lower, with green discharges.

Chafing of the skin, in children, with bilious symptoms. Ext. use, p. 126.

Cold, catarrh, when there are greenish secretions.

Diabetes; chief remedy. In health the liver so elaborates the chemical property of the sugar that on passing to the heart and by the' vena cava inferior to the lungs it turns into lactic acid. In diabetes the function of the liver is perverted, and sugar passes unchanged into the blood, and is excreted in the urine, causing great waste and destruction of tissues.

Diarrhœa, *dark bilious stools of green bile.*

Dropsy, *from liver disease; when the effused liquid is of a green colour.*

Dropsy, *scarlatinal, setting in after scarlet fever.*

Drowsiness, *often the precursor of jaundice, when there exists a greenish-grey or brownish-green tongue, or other decided bilious symptoms.*

Erysipelas ("rose"), smooth, red, shiny, coming out in blotches and with swelling of the skin. For the fever, Ferric phosphate.

Gastric derangement, with bitter taste in the mouth.

Headache, with giddiness, greenish grey coated tongue.

Intermittent fever, with vomiting of bile, tongue greenish-brown or grayish-green, with or without bitter taste.

Jaundice, arising from vexation, with bilious green evacuations, or greenish-brown coated tongue, or sallow skin.

Liver, irritable, bilious attack, too much bile, if after excessive study or mental work; also Potassium phosphate.

Polyuria simplex, excessive secretion of urine.

Preputial œdema.

Scrotal œdema.

Secretions, with or without vesicles (blisters), which are watery, and not sticky, with irritable liver.

Sick headache, with bad or bitter taste in the month, giddiness, or vomiting of bilious matter.

Skin affections, moist, with irritation and itching, and predisposition to-bilious derangements.

Skin, chafing of, with bilious symptoms.

Skin, œdematus inflammations of.

Sleepiness; see Drowsiness above.

Tongue, dirty, brownish green coating, or grayish green.

Vertigo, giddiness, dizziness, gastric derangement, with excess of bile.

Vomiting, bilious.

Vomiting, morning sickness, and bitter taste in the mouth.

Vomiting, of pure bile.

Yellow fever If it assumes the form of severe bilious remittent fever, and there is excess of bile; vomit greenish-yellow, brown, or black. Ferric phosphate for the fever in alternate doses.

12.—Silica.

The Diseases forming this group must be healed or treated with this cell-salt, as they have their seat either in the connective-tissue, the periosteum, the skin, the hair, or the nails, of which this salt is a natural constituent,

All Ailments and suppurations which are connected with the periosteum (the fibrous skin covering all bones), or those affecting the connective-tissue sheaths covering nerve-fibres; also all suppurations which are generally deep-seated, and the pus (matter) thick and yellow; with those seated on ligaments and tendons there is often very little pus. Also indurations, conditions in which swellings as of accumulated matter undergo a process of hardening.

Boils, little lumps, not mattering, blind.

Carbuncles, if intractable and very hard, or with very profuse discharge of matter. External use, page 126.

Chilblains, festering; as second remedy, if Calcium sulph. does not heal.

Dulness of hearing, with swelling and catarrh of the eustachian tubes, and of the cavity of the drum of the ear.

Ear, swelling, inflammatory, of the external meatus.

Epilepsy, nocturnal fits, at the changes of the moon.

Face-ache, with concurrent appearance of small nodules, lumps the size of a pea appearing on the scalp.

Glands, suppurating, if Calcium sulphate is not suitable.

Gouty deposits in large joints of the fingers; chalk stones are reduced by it.

Headaches, with concurrent appearance of small lumps or nodules the size of a pea on the scalp.

Hip-joint disease, to control suppuration during that process.

Indurations, hardening, as of a "stye on the eyelid," the hardening of tissues around a part formerly acutely diseased.

Injuries, neglected cases, if suppurating (festering).

Intermittent fever, some species of.

Mastitis, "weed," during suppuration, to control the formation of pus.

Perspiration of the feet, when excessive, or with heavy odour.

Secretions, mattery, bloody mattery.

Skin affections, dry eruptions, with corresponding symptoms.

Stye on the eyelid; also as a lotion to remove it, and to hasten the discharge painlessly. If there is much inflammation, about the eye, give also a few dozes of Ferric phosphate.

Suppurations (festers), having their seat in the cell-substance of the connective tissue. All deep-seated suppurations, including those on tendons, ligaments, and bone.

Suppurations, of joints, to control the formation of pus.

Swellings which become hard after threatening to suppurate.

Syphilis, chronic, with suppurations or indurations.

Tongue, induration of (hardening).

Ulcers of the lower limbs, if Calcium sulphate does not suffice.

Ulcers when deep-seated, and the periosteum is affected.

Whitlow, to control the formation of pus, and to stimulate the growth of new nails.

Wounds, when discharging thick yellow matter, where Calcium sulphate is not sufficient, and the suppuration deeper seated.

As unavoidably many technical terms are used which do not convey to the general reader their full meaning and significance, a short Glossary has been appended, which contains many terms occurring in this book dealing with the New Treatment of Disease by tissue cell salts, and in Dr. SCHÜSSLER'S pamphlet, *"The Cure of Diphtheria by Bio-chemic Treatment."*

GLOSSARY.

A

Abdomen. The lower belly, or that part of the body which lies between the thorax and the pelvis.

Abscess. A collection of pus (purulent matter) in some tissues of the body; generated by suppuration or festering; a purulent tumour.

Absorbents. Vessels which absorb or drink in, as the lacteals and lymphatics.

Acetic acid. The pure acid of vinegar, composed of two atoms carbon, with four of hydrogen, and two of oxygen ($C_2H_4O_2$).

Acid. Sharp; sour to the taste.

Aconite. Extract of the poisonous Monk's Hood, acting on the heart and circulation, the nervous system, &c.

Acrid. Sharp; pungent; bitter; of a hot, scalding nature.

Acute. Opposed to chronic; an acute disease is one which is attended with symptoms of certain degrees of severity, and comes speedily to a crisis.

Adynamic. Weak; destitute of strength through disease,

Aet: Aetas. Aged.

Aetiology. The science of the causes of diseases.

Affinity, chemical. The innate, inherent power which different bodies have of combining or uniting.

Ague. An intermittent fever, attended with cold shivering and outbreaks of heat alternately at certain defined periods.

Albumen. A substance existing abundantly in the white of an egg, and forming a constituent principle of the animal organism, consisting of carbon, hydrogen, oxygen, nitrogen, and sulphur.

Albuminoid. Like albumen; that organic basis of the cells which is composed of proteine, and constitutes part of fibrin.

Alimentary. Having the quality of nourishing. The alimentary canal is the great duct or intestine by which aliments are conveyed through the body, and the useless parts excreted.

Amenorrhœd. Suppression or delay of menstruation.

Ammonia. A chemical compound, otherwise called Volatile alkali, which in its uncombined form exists in the state of a highly pungent gas, one part nitrogen and three part hydrogen (N H8).

Amorphous. Irregular in shape; not having a determinate form.

Anæmia. A deficiency of red blood; bloodlessness; incipient loss of the vital proportion of the blood.

Analogue. One thing which resembles or corresponds with or bears great resemblance to another.

Analysis, quantitative. Consists in the determination not merely of the component parts of a compound, but their relative proportions.

Anatomy. The art of dissecting, or artificially separating the different parts of an organic body to discover their situation, structure, and economy. Morbid anatomy deals with the: structure of diseased parts.

Angina pectoris. Spasm of the heart.

Anterior Chamber of the eye lies between the cornea and iris.

Anus, The fundament, or lower opening of the body, by which excrement, evacuations, or stools are passed out of the body.

Aphtha. The thrush; a disease which shows itself in small white ulcers upon the tongue, gums, inside of the lips, and palate, common to infants.

Areolar tissue. The small (spaces) interstices of cellular tissues.

Arsenic. A virulent metallic poison. Arsenious oxide, or **White-Arsenic,** is composed of three parts oxygen to two parts-arsenic (A2 O3).

Arteries. Those blood-vessels that convey the red blood from the heart to all parts of the body, having valves only at their origin, and in this being unlike the veins, which carry the blue blood back to the heart.

Articular Rheumatism, Rheumatism of the joints.

Ascarides. A genus of intestinal worms; thread worms.

Assimilation. The taking up and converting of nutritive substances into flesh, &c, of animal bodies; the production of flesh, fat, bones, &c., from the substances supplied by food.

Assimilation, Vegetable, The process of elaboration of plant tissues from carbonic acid gas, water, ammonia compounds, and salts.

Asthma. An affection of the breathing organs characterized by difficulty of breathing recurring in paroxysms, commonly attended with cough, wheezing, and constriction of the chest.

Atrophy. Wasting away of the body, arising from defective nutrition.

Attenuation. Subdivision; the reduction of a drug by dilution or-pulverization,

B

Base. In chemistry that substance with which an acid unites to form a salt. The leading substance of compounds.

Belladonna. Deadly Nightshade.

Bile. A thin yellow bitter liquor, separated from the blood in the liver, collected in the gall bladder, and thence discharged by the common duct.

Bilious. Subject to excessive secretion of bile; an overflow of bile causes a bitter taste in the mouth, and is usually accompanied by drowsiness or severe vomiting. In extreme cases when the liver is affected the eyeballs become yellow, and the disease takes the form of jaundice, often with suppression of this secretion.

Bio-chemic. Pertaining to the chemistry of life; the chemical actions taking place in the body in life, by which one class of substances conjoin with certain others, by the laws of combination and chemical affinity, to form new compounds, such combinations acquiring new properties. This takes place only between dissimilar particles, as seen between certain organic and certain inorganic substances.

Biology. The science which investigates the phenomena of animal and vegetable life.

Bladder, paralysis of the, applies to the sphincter muscles; causing inability of retaining the urine, generally of old people.

Blind boil. A swelling, attended by inflammation of the part, containing little pus, and mostly blood.

Bone-earth. Phosphate of lime; the earthy substance of bone.

Bright's disease. A disease of the kidneys and the urinary organs, with albumen in the urine.

Bronchi. The ramifications of the trachea or windpipe; the bronchial tubes which branch from the trachea and carry air into the lungs.

Bronchitis. An inflammation of the lining membrane of the windpipe or bronchial tubes.

Bronchocele. Enlargement of the thyroid gland at windpipe; goitre; cellular sarcoma.

Buboes. Hard swelling of the glands of the groin and arm-pit through venereal or other causes.

Bursa of the knee-cap. A small serous sac found between bony surfaces moving upon each other, and thus ensuring their free and easy movement.

Butyric acid. A colourless acid found in butter, and also occurring in the gastric juice, perspiration, urine, etc. It consists of four atoms of carbon, eight of hydrogen, and two of oxygen ($C_4 H_8 O_2$).

C

Calcareous. Partaking of the nature of lime; containing lime.

Calcium, The metallic base of lime.

Callus. The new growth of bony matter between the extremities-of fractured bones, serving to unite them.—Callous. A hardness of any part of the body which should be soft in its natural condition, as of the skin from friction or from swelling.

Cancer. A hard or ulcerating virulent tumour, arising mostly from constitutional weakness. There are four varieties of the disease: (1) Colloid cancer, a soft tumour, found principally in the stomach and alimentary canal, and containing a grayish, glue-like secretion. (2) Encephaloid cancer, a soft tumour, which frequently bleeds, and is distinguished by its vessel-like roots. (3) Scirrhous cancer, a hard tumour, often painless. (4) Epilthelial cancer, a skin tumour, secreting a thin yellow fluid. The disease in all its varieties is often fatal.

Canker. Certain small corroding ulcers in the mouth, particularly of children or nursing mothers.

Cantharides. The Spanish fly, used, when dry, for making blisters, &c.

Capillaries. Small hair-like tubes; minute blood vessels existing in almost all parts of the body, of which there are many so minute as to be only the 5000th part of an inch in thickness. Through these the blood corpuscles have to circulate.

Capsular ligament. A cup-like arrangement of connective tissue, usually found surrounding ball and socket joints.

Carbon. Pure charcoal; an elementary, combustible substance, black, brittle, light, and inodorous. It may be obtained from most organic matters, animal as well as vegetable, by ignition, in close vessels.

Carbonate. A compound formed by the union of carbonic acid with a base.

Carbonic acid gas. A compound of one atom of carbon and two atoms-of oxygen (CO_2); it is gaseous and colourless; given off from the lungs in breathing, and if allowed to accumulate in a confined space inducing suffocation.

Carbuncle. An inflammatory suppurating tumour, or painful boil or ulcer.

Cardiac. Pertaining to the heart.

Cartilage. Gristle; solid elastic substance attached to bone, softer than bone.

Cartilage salt. Sodium chloride, met with in the cells of cartilage or gristle, which is a smooth solid substance or tissue, softer than bone, but harder than a ligament, without cavities for marrow, &c.

Catamenia. The menses; monthly flow; menstruation.

Cataract. A disease of the eye, non-transparency or opacity of the crystaline lens, causing loss of sight.

Catarrh. Inflamed state of the mucous membrane of the air passages, more particularly of that portion which lines the nostrils, producing; among other symptoms, an increased defluxion of mucus from the nose.

Catarrh (common) is popularly called a cold.

Catarrh (epidemic) is termed influenza.

Caustic. A substance which burns or disorganises animal bodies when brought into contact with them.

Cauterizing. The act of burning with a cautery or caustic.

Cell. A little bag or minute bladder containing fluid or other substances.

Cellular. Consisting of an infinite number of minute cells, as the cellular tissues and membranes in animal bodies.

Cell salts. The inorganic mineral or saline substances which are the essential component parts of the cells, of which tissues consist, and may, therefore, be called tissue cell salts, or simply tissue salts.

Centigramme. The hundereth part of a gramme. The gramme is the unit of weights in the Metric system, and is equal to 15.432 grains.

Cephalalgic Relating to headaches.

Cephalitis. Inflammation of the brain.

Cephalotomata. Blood tumours. Soft vascular tumours on the parietal bones of new-born children.

Cerebral. Pertaining to the brain.

Chalk stones. Deposit of sodium urate, forming whitish concretions on the joints in the hands and feet of persons afflicted with gout.

Chancre. A venereal or syphilitic ulcer.

Chemical affinity. The force which holds together the elements in a compound, and which determines the combination of different substances to form compounds, an operation exemplified in the absorption of the tissue salts into the particular cells where they are required, and where in a state of perfect health they are found to exist in proper proportions.

Chemistry is an extensive science, the objects of which are to investigate the composition of all kinds of matter, and their mutual actions, combinations, and decompositions.

Chilblains. Redness, sometimes with swelling on the hands or feet from cold in winter, giving rise to tingling, itching, and pain.

Chloride. A compound of chlorine with another element, such as sodium, potassium, &c.

Chlorine. A greenish-yellow gas, obtained from common salt.

Chloroform. A fluid obtained by distilling chloride of lime with alcohol or methylated spirits, and now largely employed to produce insensibility to pain during an operation. It contains carbon, hydrogen, and chlorine in these proportions (C H Ch3).

Chlorosis. The green sickness, a disease incident to young females, giving them a pale, greenish hue; excess of white blood corpuscles.

Chlorotic condition. Affected by chlorosis, or green sickness, a disease incident to young females, giving them a pale greenish hue.

Cholera—English. A disease characterized by vomiting and purging, with great pain, debility, and crampy pain.

Cholera—Asiatic. Known in Europe since 1817. All the symptoms are more violent than the former, with violent choleraic cramps, biliary disturbance, purging, stools like rice-water, great prostration, and collapse.

Chondroma. A cartilaginous growth seated in the periosteum covering the bone.

Chorea. St. Vitus' dance, a disease which manifests itself in convulsive motions of the limbs, causing strange and involuntary gesticulations.

Chromatopsia. Spasmodic visions of rainbow colours.

Chronic. Of long continuance; lingering; in contra-distinction to acute.

Chyle. A milky fluid formed by the action of the pancreatic juice and the bile on the chyme after leaving the stomach, which, being absorbed by the lacteal ducts, is poured into the blood.

Chyme. The condition of food, after being dissolved by the gastric juices, and before it is converted into chyle.

Cicatrization. The process of healing or forming a cicatrice; a scar; the state of being healed, cicatrized, or skinned over.

Clinical. Applied to a discourse on the disease of a patient at his bedside to students; also to notes of a case so visited, and subsequently read or published.

Coagulate. To solidify, as when blood changes into a liver-like mass.

Colic. A spasmodic painful disorder of the bowels (various kinds), attended with severe crampy pain.

Collapse. Sinking; a sudden and extreme depression of strength; failure of vital power; utter prostration.

Commotio-cerebri. Disturbance of brain functions.

Compress. Folds of soft linen cloth or lint, used to cover the dressings of wounds, &c.

Concomitant. Accompanying; conjoined with.

Condylomata. Warty excrescences, or soft, fleshy, indolent excrescence.

Congestion. An accumulation of blood in capillaries or other blood vessels in any part of the body; a relaxed condition arising from want of normal tensity in the muscular fibres of the blood vessels, caused by insufficiency of iron.

Conjunctiva palpebrarum. The fine, sensitive membrane which line the eyelids, and is joined on to the ball of the eye.

Conjunctivitis. Inflammation of the lining membrane of the eyelid facing the eye.

Connective tissue is found in the animal body as a supporting framework and investment to various organs, besides being intimately interwoven with all the textures of the body. It is composed of cells and intercellular gelatine-yielding substance.

Constipation. Costiveness; defective excretion of fæces or stools.

Contra functional. Out of working order.

Convalesence. The slow recovery of health and strength after disease.

Convulsions. Violent and involuntary contractions of the muscular parts of an animal body; spasm; agitation; commotion.

Co-ordinating. All parts of a machine working towards the same object, and keeping up the cosmic order of the body.

Cornea. Transparent horny membrane in front of the pupil of the eye.

Corpuscle. A minute body or physical atom seen only by the microscope. There are nearly 3,000,000 corpuscles in one droplet of our blood. These globules carry the iron (cell salt) to all parts of the body by the circulation of the blood; hence the reasonableness of using infinitesimal quantities of cell salts. One corpuscle does not exceed the 120,000,000,000th of a cubic inch.

Corrugated. Wrinkled; furrowed; uneven.

Coryza. A limpid, ropy, mucous discharge from the nose, generally caused by cold in the head.

Cramp. A spasmodic contraction of the muscles, attended generally with much pain, arising from various causes.

Cranial tabes. A wasting away of the bones of the skull.

Croup. Inflammation and exudation of thick, tough phlegm at the top of the trachea of windpipe, accompanied by a hoarse cough and difficult respiration; especially incident to children.

Group, hysterical, is attended with spasms of the muscles of the windpipe.

Crusta lactea. Scald head of children; scabs.

Crystalline lens, in the eye. A doubly convex, transparent, solid body, with a rounded circumference, lying behind the iris in the partition between the aqueous and vitreous humours.

Cupped. Bled; blood taken from the body by means of the cupping-glass.

Cuticle. The scarf-skin; the thin outer coat of the skin; also-called epidermis.

D

Dandruff. A white or yellow scurf which forms on the head, and comes off in small scales or particles.

Decomposition. The breaking up of a chemical compound into its elements, or into two or more less complex compounds.

Defluxion. A flowing off or discharge of humours, as from the nose.

Delirium. A state in which the ideas of a person are wild, irregular and unconnected; a wandering of the mind; disorder of the intellect.

Delirium tremens. An affection of the brain, with illusions of the mind, trembling of the body, produced by excessive use of spiritous liquors in large or repeated small doses, which gradually deprive the brain pulp of its proper softness and moisture, and harden it.

Dentition. The breeding or cutting of first or second teeth.

Desqumation. Free scaling of skin; the separation of the outer skin in small scales.

Diabetes millitus. An excessive and morbid discharge of urine containing saccharine matter.

Diagnosis. Distinguishing one disease from another by its symptoms.

Diarrhœa. Violent purging.

Diathesis. Particular disposition of constitution.

Dilatation. Extension or relaxation of muscular fibres.

Diphtheritis. Diphtheria; the disease of the throat, in which there is a formation of a false membrane, in fatal cases producing suffocation.

Diplopia. Seeing double; an affection of the eye.

Dissipated. Scattered; dispersed.

Dorsal. Pertaining to the back; hence Tabes dorsalis, wasting of the spinal cord.

Dropsy. A morbid collection of water in the cellular tissues or other cavities of the body.

Duodenal. Relating to the duodenum, the first of the small intestines immediately following the stomach; the twelve inch intestine.

Duodenitis. Inflammation of the duodenum, the first part of the intestines, commencing at the small or pyloric end of the stomach. It is capable of considerable distension.

Dynamics. The science which treats of the laws of force, moving power, matter in motion, mechanics.

Dynamic. Relating to dynamics.

Dysentery. A flux in which the stools consist chiefly of blood and mucus, or other morbid matter, accompanied with griping of the bowels, and followed by tenesmus (a straining; a painful feeling for evacuation).

Dysmenorrhœa. Difficult or painful menstruation or period.

Dyspepsia. Bad digestion; indigestion; the imperfect conversion of food into nourishment.

Dyspnœa. A difficulty or shortness of breathing.

Dysury. Difficulty of voiding the urine (different from ischury) or suppression.

E

Eczema. An eruption of the skin; sometimes small vesicles on, or morbid redness of, the skin.

Effete. Having lost the power of production; worn out.

Effusion. A pouring out; what is poured out.

Elastic cells. Those cells which constitute elastic tissues of the living-body.

Element. That which cannot be divided by chemical analysis, and therefore considered as a simple substance.

Eliminate. To expel; to discharge; to throw off; to set at liberty.

Emaciation. Thinness produced by the gradual wasting away of the flesh of the body.

Empyema. A collection of purulent matter, chiefly in the cavity of the pleura (a thin membrane which covers the interior of the lungs).

Encephalitis, Inflammation of the brain.

Encephaloid-cancer. Soft or water cancer. Curable under bio-chemic treatment.

Enteralgia. Nervous pain in the stomach.

Enteritis, Inflammation of the bowels.

Enuresis. Incontinence of urine; involuntary flow of urine at night.

Epidermis. The upper layer of the integument, the cuticle or scarf skin of the body.

Epigastric, or upper part of the abdomen, where digestion takes place.

Epilepsy. The falling sickness; a disease characterized by spasms or convulsions and loss of sense.

Epistaxis. Bleeding from the nose; nasal hæmorrhage.

Epithelial sheathings. Portions of the layer of cells forming the inner membraneous surface of the bladder, etc.

Epithelioma. Cancer on a mucus lining, with discharge of thin yellow watery mattery sticky secretions.

Eructations. Ejection of wind from the stomach through the mouth.

Erysipelas. Rose; St. Anthony's fire; an inflammatory affection of some part of the skin, smooth or blistering.

Erysipelatous. Eruptive; resembling erysipelas, or partaking of its nature.

Eustachian tubes. Small canals or ducts running from cavities of the inner ear into the back part of the mouth.

Excoriation. Abrasion, ruffling, or destruction of the skin, causing soreness.

Excretion. The throwing off of effete matter, &c.

Exostosis. A bony tumour; a tumour of the bone.

Extensor. Any muscle of the body that extends or straightens a part; opposed to flexor.

Extrayasated blood. The blood of the body escaped from its natural canals, &c., and consequent diffusion in the surrounding tissue, as from the rupture of a blood-vessel.

Exudation. Discharge of some parts of the blood plasma from the mucous lining and other tissues, in a diseased state.

F

Fæces. Evacuations; stools.

Fascii. The thin tendinous coverings which surround the muscles of the limbs and bind them in their places.

Febrile. Pertaining to fever; feverish.

Fetid. Having an offensive smell.

Fibrin. A white, fibrous, albumenoid substance obtained from blood.

Fits. Paroxysms of diseases; sudden and violent attacks; convulsions.

Flatulent. Windy; affected with air or gas generated in the stomach and intestines.

Fluoride. A compound of fluorine with another element—*e.g.* Calcium fluoride (Ca. F2).

Flux. In pathology, an extraordinary abnormal issue or evacuation. Fomentation. External application of hot moist flannels, &c, to ease-pain or excite action.

Fontanelles. The soft cartilaginous membrane at the top of an infant's head.

Frontal. Pertaining to the forehead (Lat. *frons*).

Function. The office of, or purpose subserved by, any given organ or part of an animal or plant.

Fungi. An important class of vegetable forms characterised by the absence of chlorophyll (green colouring matter), and requiring organic compounds as nourishment, such as the diphtheritic exudation; others, as mushrooms and toad-stools, grow on leaf soil or the barks of trees; while others again, as moulds and yeasts, make their appearance in vegetable juices or saccharine, solutions. Some, as rust and smut, are parasitic.

Furuncle. A boil; a superficial suppurating tumour.

G

Gall bladder. A small membraneous sac, shaped like a pear, which is attached to the liver, and receives an extremely bitter' fluid, called gall or bile, from the liver.

Ganglion. A hard, round, indolent swelling, of the colour of the skin, situated on a tendon, varying in size from that of a pea to that of an egg. It consists of a fluid contained in a cyst of greater or less thickness, such as is sometimes met with on the back of the Wrist. This term ganglion is also employed to denote an enlargement in the course of a nerve, and constituting a nerve centre.

Gangrenous. Mortified; indicating mortification of living flesh.

Gastric. Belonging to the stomach.

Gastritis. Acute inflammation of the stomach.

Germ. Seed; first principle; the ovum.

Gland. An organ of the body in which a secretion of some kind is-elaborated from the blood—*e.g.* lymphatic sweat glands, salivary, glands, gastric glands.

Glossopharyngeus and lingualis. A nerve connected with the pharynx and the tongue.

Gluten. The nitrogenous proximate element of certain food stuffs, and one of its most nutritive parts.

Glycerine. The sweet principle of oils and fats.

Gonorrhœa. A contagious inflammation of the genital organs, attended with a profuse secretion of mucus, &c.

Gout. An inflammatory disease of certain joints, chiefly of the hands and feet, with chalky deposits; attacks occurring by paroxysms.

Granule. A small particle; a little grain.

Gravel. A disease produced by small calculous concretions in the kidneys and bladder.

Glauber Salt. Sodium sulphate.

H

Hæmatemesis. Vomiting of blood.

Hæmaturia. Bloody urine.

Hæmorrhage. A discharge of blood through rupture of blood vessels.

Hæmorrhoids. Piles; small tumours in different stages of congestion, and inflammation within or outside the anus.

Hawking. Making an effort to discharge phlegm from the throat

Hay asthma, or hay fever, summer catarrh, caused by the seeds of grasses.

Hernia. A rupture of the peritoneum, with protusion of part of the bowels.

Herpes. Shingles; large or small blebs, in patches on the skin.

Herpes-zoster. A spreading eruption encircling one half of the body.

Heterogeneous. Of a different kind or nature; unlike or dissimilar in nature.

Hip-joint disease. Scrofulous affection commencing with inflammation around the hip-joint. The pain is often felt for a long time before swelling sets in, with ultimate discharge of matter from an abcess on the part; the head of the bone also becomes implicated.

Histology. The microscopic study of the tissues of the body.

Homœopathy. A medical practice the opposite of Allopathy.

Homogeneous. Of the same kind or nature.

Hooping cough. An affection of the bronchi and breathing apparatus, attended with repeated spasmodic, convulsive fits of cough, ending in a characteristic whoop.

Hordeolum. A stye, or small tumour of the eyelid, so called from Hordeum, a barleycorn.

Housemaid's-knee. A watery tumour; enlargement of bursa or sac on the knee-cap.

Hydrocele. (In the male) Dropsy in the scrotum.

Hydrocephalus. Dropsy in the head, or water in the head.

Hydrogen. One of the constituent elements of water; a colourless combustible gas, and the lightest substance known.

Hygroma. A watery tumour.

Hyperemia. Excess of blood in any part; accumulation. Hypertrophy. Unnatural morbid enlargement of an organ of the body.

Hypochondriasis. Depression of spirits, with languor, listlessness, and despair of recovery as the result of long continued indigestion. especially affection of the lining membrane of the stomach.

Hypopium. Hypopion; an effusion of pus into the anterior chamber of the eye.

Hysteria. A nervous affection of women, attended with involuntary laughter and crying.

Hysteric. Disordered in the region of the womb; troubled with fits or nervous affections.

Humid. Moist; damp; somewhat wet or watery.

I

Ichor. Thin watery serous fluid oozing from an ulcer.

Idiopathic. An inherent, morbid, or diseased state, not produced by any preceding disease or injury.

Imbibition. A drinking in; the passage of fluid or gaseous matter into and through the tissues. Endosmosis.

Incineration. The act of reducing to ashes.

Incontinence. The inability of any of the animal organs to restrain discharges of their contents.

Indication. Any symptom or occurrence in a disease, which serves to direct to suitable remedies.

Induration. The act of hardening.

Inertia. That property of matter whereby it tends to continue at rest or to move when in motion. Indisposition to move.

Infiltration. The entering of a fluid into the pores of a body.

Infinitesimal. An infinitely small quantity,

Inherent. Existing in, so as to be almost inseparable from; innate; inborn.

Inorganic, mineral. Devoid of organs; not possessing the organs or instruments of life.

Insectivorous. Feeding or subsisting on insects.

Integument. That which naturally invests or covers another thing, as the skin covers the body.

Intercostal. Lying between the ribs.

Intercurrent. Running between or among; intervening.

Intermittent. A term applied to any disease that entirely ceases at certain intervals, and then returns.

Interstice. A narrow or small space between things closely set; hence intersticial.

Intertrigo. A species of erythema, redness of skin, induced by acridity of the urine; scalded.

Intestines. The bowels or lower part of the alimentary canal; a muslcular canal or tube extending from the stomach to the anus, about twenty-six feet in length; hence intestinal.

Irritation. The operation of exciting excess. (In physiology; a vitiated and abnormal state of sensation or action produced by external or mechanical agents or influences; the morbid super-excitation of vitality or function).

Irritation-Hypenemia. Excess of blood through irritation or stimulation in any part of the body; stasis or accumulation of blood.

Ischury. A stoppage or suppression of urine.

Itis. To force; urge against; denoting violent action in the blood vessels; used as a terminal to indicate inflammation.

Jaundice. A disease of a biliary nature, characterized by yellowness of the eyes, skin, and urine, &c.

K

Kidney disease (Bright's). See Bright's disease.

Kidneys. Two organs of the body, the function of which is to secrete the urine, this fluid afterwards flowing from them into the bladder.

King's evil. Scrofula.

L

Lachrymose. Readily shedding tears; tendency to crying.

Lacteals. The lymphatics of the intestines; minute vessels which absorb the chyle and convey it to the thoracic duct, and so into the blood at the junction of the left subclavian and jugular veins.

Lactic acid. An organic acid present when milk has turned sour.

Laryngismus stridulus. Millar's asthma of children; child crowing, from partial obstruction of the windpipe; rickety children are especially liable to such attacks.

Larynx. The upper part of the windpipe; a cartilaginous cavity.

Lassitude. A morbid sensation of languor, frequently preceding and accompanying disease.

Leucorrhœa. A discharge from the uterus; vulgarly called the "Whites."

Lichen. A papular cutaneous eruption of red pimples, like goose-skin reddened, with a pricking sensation and itching.

Ligaments. Tough flexible bands of connective tissue which bind the bones together at the joints.

Liver. A large abdominal organ, of a deep red colour, lying under the false ribs on the right side; its principal use is to secrete the bile.

Local. Limited or confined to a spot or place.

Lockjaw. A violent rigid contraction of the muscles of the jaw, by which its motion is suspended; tetanus.

Lumbago. An acute pain in the loins and small of the back; a rheumatic affection of the muscles of the loins.

Lumbar region. That portion of the back between the false ribs and the upper edge of the haunch-bone.

Lunar-caustic. Fused nitrate of silver.

Lungs. The organs of respiration, which, with the heart, completely fill the thoracic cavity or chest; the right is divided into three, the left into two, lobes. The upper lobes are most prone to disease.

Lupus. A tubercular disease of the face and nose.

Lymph. Watery humour, or a colourless fluid, allied to the serum of blood, and carried through the body by vessels called lymphatics.

M

Macrocosm. The infinitely large or visible horizon.

Magnesium. The metallic base of magnesia.

Malaise. An indefinite feeling of uneasiness; being ill at ease, not at all well.

Malignant. Virulent; dangerous.

Mamme, The breasts of a female.

Manganese. A hard brittle metal, of a greyish-white colour.

Mania transitoria. Temporary insanity, due to an excess of blood on the brain.

Marrow. A soft oleaginous substance contained in the cavities of animal bones.

Mastitis. Inflammation or suppuration of the breasts of women.

Measles. A contagious disease (Rubeola) indicated by a pinkish rash upon the skin. Ushered in, like influenza, with watery eyes.

Meatus. A passage, as that leading to the ear, called the meatus auditorius.

Megrim, Migraine. A neuralgic pain in the side of the head, *i.e.,* one-sided, often periodical.

Melancholia. Lowness of spirits; mental depression; often accompanied by irritability of the liver.

Membrane. A thin, white, flexible skin, formed by fibres interwoven like network, and serving to cover some parts of the body. Mucous membrane, inside lining of hollow cavities, such as mouth, throat, etc.

Meninges. The two membranes that envelop the brain.

Meningitis. Inflammation of the meninges, or membranes of the brain, or of the spinal cord.

Menstrual colic. A spasmodic and painful affection of the bowels, but especially the colon, during the monthly period.

Menstruation. Menses; the catamenial period or monthly discharge of women.

Mercury. Quicksilver; a metal used in medicine; a very subtile and powerful drug.

Mesentery. A membrane in the cavity of the abdomen attached to the vertebrae of the loins. It encloses and sustains the bowels; hence mesenteric.

Metabolism. Chemical changes in the living body; pertaining to vital affinity.

Metamorphosis. Change of condition, form, or shape.

Metritis. Inflammation of the womb, pain, swelling, tenderness, vomiting, difficulty of passing water.

Microcosm. The infinitely small; the miniature world.

Micturition. Passing urine.

Milligramme. The thousandth part of the French gramme, and equal in Imperial weight to about 1/70 of a grain Troy. Though small, yet even this quantity of cell-salt has effect.

Molecule. A name given to the minute particles of which bodies are composed. Means strictly the smallest quantity of an element or of a compound that can exist in a free state.

Morbid. Diseased; sickly; unhealthy; unsound.

Morphia. The chief narcotic principle of opium.

Mortification. Death of one part of the body while the rest is alive; gangrene.

Mortify. To destroy the organic texture and vital functions of some part of a living animal.

Motor. A mover; in anatomy applied to certain nerves which control certain muscles and their movements.

Mucous lining. A membraneous lining of the canals and cavities of the body, as the throat, stomach, intestines, &c.

Mucus. A viscid fluid, secreted by the mucous membrane.

Mumps. A swelling of the parotid glands situated below the ear.

Muriatic acid, or Hydrochloric acid. A strongly corrosive acid comlposed of one equivalent of hydrogen and one of chlorine.

Muscles, Flesh. Such parts of the fleshy portion of the body as perform movements by contracting or relaxing. Voluntary muscles, those subject to the will, as of the face, arm, leg, &c. Involuntary muscles, as the heart, stomach, &c.

Myosin, An albuminoid body extracted from muscular fibre; muscle-juice.

Myositis. Inflammation of the muscles.

N

Nausea. Originally sea-sickness; disposition to vomit.

Nebulous. Cloudy; hazy.

Nephritis. Inflammation of the kidneys.

Nettle rash. An eruption of the skin, much resembling that produced by the sting of a nettle.

Neuralgia. Excessive pains darting along the track of a nerve. (Rheumatism of the nerve, as sciatica, &c.)

Neurilemma (Nerve sheaths). The membrane which invests the substance of the nerves, and forms for each filament a distinct sheath which may be easily separated in the form of a tube.

Nidus. A nest.

Nitrate of silver. Nitric acid, saturated with pure silver.

Nitrogen. An elementary gas which forms the base of nitric acid, and composes four-fifths of our atmosphere, acting as a diluent of the-oxygen.

Nodules. Rounded little lumps or tumours arising from the swelling-of the periosteum or membrane covering the surface of the bone.

Noma, Water canker. Eating, corroding, or cancerous sores attacking; the cheek and skin, and the vulva of women.

Nomenclature. A vocabulary of names or technical terms of things in any art or science.

Non-assimilation. Food taken and not converted into nourishment, nor absorbed by the tissues of the body.

Non-functional. Not performing its functions; not in working order.

Normal. Natural; according to rule; not deviating from the ordinary structure. In anatomy, healthy.

O

Œdema of the ankles. A local dropsical swelling; hence œdematous;

Œdema pulmonarium. Swelling or infiltration of the lungs with serous phlegmy humour.

Œsophagus. The gullet; the canal through which food and drink pass to the stomach.

Orchitis. Inflammation of the testicles, the seminal glands in the male.

Organic. Relating to all structures possessing organs or instruments through which natural activities are made manifest.

Organism. A living thing having organs, *e.g.,* any animal or vegetable-forms.

Organic substance. A living or organised substance which is readily subject to change in its structure from putrifaction, decomposiltion, or otherwise. It thus differs from the substances of the-mineral kingdom or inorganic matter, such as lime, iron, etc.

Osseous. Composed of bone; resembling bone.

Ostitis. Inflammation of the bone.

Otitis. Inflammation of the ear.

Ovarian. Relating to the ovaries and womb.

Ovarian neuralgia. Relating to the ovaries, whence the ova pass-through the Fallopian tubes into the womb.

Oxidation. The burning away of any substance in oxygen, that is, oxygen entering into mechanical combination with another substance.

Oxygen. An electro-negative, basifying, and acidifying elementary principle; the vital part of the atmosphere, and the supporter of ordinary combustion.

Ozena. An ulcer of the nose, discharging fetid purulent matter, and sometimes even affecting the bone, met with in scrofulus constitutions.

P

Palpitation, Excessive beating of the heart.

Pancreas. The sweet-bread, a glandular organ situated at the bottom of the stomach, reaching from the liver on the right to the spleen on the left side of the body.

Paralysis. Loss of motion, or sensation, affecting the nerves of one or more parts of the body; special kind, called palsy.

Parasitic. Growing and living upon some other organism.

Parietal Pertaining to or within the sides of anything; thus the parietal bones form the sides and upper part of the skull

Parotid. Pertaining to the two glands, one on each side of the ear, which secrete a portion of the saliva.

Patella. The knee-pan, or knee-cap.

Pathology. That part of medicine which treats of the cause, nature, and symptoms of diseases.

Pathogenetic. Treating of the causes of disease.

Pemphigus. An eruption of bullæ; watery vesicles or blebs, red at their base, attended with feverishness.

Pericarditis. Inflammation of the membraneous covering of the heart.

Periosteum. Fibrous membrane which covers all bones.

Periostitis. Inflammation of the periosteum.

Peritonitis. Inflammation of the peritoneum or thin serous membrane lining the internal surface of the abdomen; also called inflammation of the side.

Perturbation. Agitation; disturbance.

Phagedenic. A spreading, sloughing ulcer; gangrenous.

Pharmacology. Science of preparing medicines.

Pharyngitis. Inflammation of the pharynx or upper part of the gullet.

Phenomena. Appearances. Usually applied to those appearances or symptoms of disease of which the cause is not immediately obvious.

Phlebitis. Inflammation of the veins, tenderness, heat, redness, and' knots in their course. It may follow wounds, operations, or labour.

Phlegm. Mucous matter; watery fluid; bronchial mucus; viscide matter ejected from the throat.

Phosphate. A salt of phosphoric acid; a combination of phosphoric acid with a base, such as lime, potass, &c.

Phosphoric acid. An acid composed of one equivalent of Phosphorus,. three of Hydrogen, and four of Oxygen (H_3PO_4).

Phosphorus. An elementary substance obtained from bone, of a waxlike consistency, highly combustible, of a yellowish colour, and semi-transparent.

Phrenitis. Inflammation of the brain, attended with fever and dellirium; frenzy.

Physics applied. Practical application of the properties of matter; the laws of motion as found to exist in nature.

Physico-chemical. Natural or material productions in the body by natural agents, in harmony with the principles of chemistry.

Physiology. The study of the operations which take place in living or organized beings.

Plasma. The colourless fluid part of the blood in which the corpuscles float; liquor sanguinis; contains most of the chlorine and soda-of the blood.

Plastic. A mass of matter capable of being moulded into a definite-form, as the diphtheritic exudation.

Pleurisy. An inflammation of the pleura or thin membrane which covers the lungs and lines the inside of the chest or thorax.

Plexus. Network; in anatomy applied to blood vessels, nerves, or fibres; a close network of nerves or blood vessels.

Polypus. A tumour of morbid growth, attached by its roots, thin ends or stalk, to some mucous membrane.

Polyuria. An excessive passing of urine, as in diabetes insipidus, which is devoid of sugar.

Post-scarlatinal dropsy. A morbid collection of water in any part of the body after scarlatina.

Potassium. The metallic base of potash.

Precursory. Preceding; the forerunner, as precursory chills.

Premonitory. Stage in which occur forewarning symptoms.

Preputial. Pertaining to the foreskin.

Proud flesh. The name of a spongy, fungoid excrescence formed in wounds.

Psychology. The science which treats of the soul, or thinking faculties, as distinguished from *physiology,* which treats of the visible body.

Puerperal. Belonging to child-birth; hence puerperal fever, childbed fever occurring soon after parturition. Puerperal convulsions.

Punctae lachrymosa. Tear punctures; small apertures which perforate each papilla lachrymale or minute soft prominence in the corner of the eye near the nose.

Purgative. Purging, cathartic, drastic; hence to purge. The term purging is at times substituted for diarrhœa, dysentery, and looseness of the bowels.

Purulent. Consisting of pus or corrupt matter, contained in ulcers, &c.

Pus. Yellowish white matter, found in abscesses or boils, &c.

Pustules. Little pimples or blisters; small elevations of the skin, containing matter.

Putrid. In a state of decomposition or disorganization; corrupt; rotten.

Pyrosis. A derangement of the stomach, attended with a sensation of burning; the waterbrash; heartburn.

Q

Quinsy. A suppurative inflammation of the tonsils of the throat, with yellow matter forming.

R

Rachitis. Soft state of the bones in children, called Rickets.

Raisonnement. Reasoning.

Rale. A rattling or wheezing in the throat; every kind of noise attending the breathing in the bronchia and vesicles of the lungs different from the sound of breathing in health.

Ramify. To divide into branches.

Resolution. In medicine, the dispersion and disappearance of inflammatory affections of the system.

Retching. Attempt to vomit.

Retinitis. Inflammation of the retina, the pulpy expansion of the optic nerve, resembling network, in the interior of the eye.

Rheumatic fever. Acute rheumatism, accompanied by intense fever.

Rheumatism. A painful disease affecting the muscles and joints, acute, called articular rheumatism. There are other varieties, as lumbago, which occurs in the loins.

Rupia. An eruptive disease, characterised by broad, flat vesicles, the scales being easily rubbed off, yet recurring.

Rupture. The breaking or bursting, as of a blood vessel. See Hernia.

S

Saccharated. Mixed with, or containing sugar.

Salicylic acid. An acid obtained from the distilled products of willow-bark (salix), poplar-bark, and other similar sources, and largely used as an anti-septic. It is composed of carbon, hydrogen, and oxygen, in three proportions ($C_7 H_6 O_8$).

Saliva. Spittle; the fluid secreted by the salivary glands.

Salivation. An excessive flow of saliva, sometimes from the bad effects of mercury.

Salt. A compound resulting from the mutual action of an acid and an alkali or a base.

Scarlet fever. Scarlatina; a febrile disease characterized by an eruption of crimson red patches appearing on the chird day, first on the fauces and breast.

Sciatica. A rheumatic affection of the hip joint and sciatic nerve; a neuralgic pain along the whole course of the sciatic nerve from the hip to the knee.

Scirrhus. A hard tumour on any part of the body; the induration or hardening of a gland ending in cancer.

Scorbutic Affected or diseased with scurvy.

Scrofula. A disease affecting the glands; the King's evil.

Scrotum. The sac containing the testicles; hence scrotal.

Scurvy. A disease attended by livid spots, debility, spongy gums, &c, occasioned by a limited range of food deficient of potassium chloride.

Secondary symptoms. Sequelæ; morbid affections following acute diseases.

Secretion. A separating of the animal fluids by various organs; hence secretory glands.

Septic. Having power to promote putrefaction.

Serum. The watery liquid part of the blood, like whey, which separates from the blood corpuscles on coagulation.

Shingles (Herpes Zoster). An eruption round the trunk or round the armpit, characterized by vesicles or small blisters, attended by inflammation of the parts, and considerable pain.

Silica. An important constituent of rocks. Quartz, flint, and sand are natural forms of Silica.

Sinew. Tendon; that which unites muscle to bone.

Sloughing. The dead structure of flesh that separntes from the living parts, as from a wound or sore.

Smallpox (Variola). An infectious febrile disease, accompanied with eruption on the skin, which is at first hard, red, and pointed, and at the third day assumes a bladder-like appearance.

Sodium. The metallic base of soda.

Sodium sulphate (Glauber's salt). First discovered as a separate salt by Glauber by the distillation of common salt over the oil of vitriol. It is found in a natural state in many localities efflorescent on the soil, or dissolved in mineral springs, salt lakes, and salt mines. The following is the composition of this substance found in its artificial separation (N2 S O4). All the separate chemical component parts which go to make up this salt are found in the tissues of the body, and in essential food stuffs.

Sodium urate. A compound of soda and uric acid—a white, tasteless, and inodorous acid carried off in urine—when deposited about the joints gives rise to gout.

Sopor. Sleepiness; drowsiness; a heavy sleep.

Sordes. Foul, dirty deposit on the teeth during disease.

Spasms. Sudden and violent contractions of one or more muscles; cramps.

Spectrum analysis. The art of ascertaining the character and composition of bodies when in a state of combustion, by causing rays of light from the body desired to be so analysed to pass through a prism, each substance having its own characteristic system of lines. This method is adopted to ascertain the qualitative or quantitative analysis of minerals, &c., when the presence of extremely minute quantities of different bodies has to be determined.

Spermatic. Consisting of animal seed; seminal.

Sphincter. A muscle that contracts or shuts an orifice or opening round which it is placed.

Spinal cord. The grayish white matter, a continuation of the brain substance or matter lodged in the interior of the spinal column or backbone.

Spleen. The milt situated on the posterior of the left hypochondrium, near the large end of the stomach.

Spleenitis. Inflammation of the spleen, the ductless gland situated at the large end of the stomach, composed of arcolar tissue.

Sprain. To overstrain the muscles or ligaments of a joint.

Stasis. Stagnation of the blood, or accumulation of the blood.

Stertorus. Applied to the loud snoring, as in appoplexy and diphtheria.

Stomach, proper, is the membraneous bag and principal organ of digestion, into which the food passes from the mouth. Pain in the stomach proper, however, is termed indigestion pain.

Stomach-ache. Often conventionally referred to pains in the lower region of the abdomen or belly.

Stomatitis. Inflammation or ulcers of the mouth.

Strabismus. Squinting.

Stricture. The narrowing of a channel or canal of the body, as of the gullet, lower bowel, or urethra.

Strumous. Scrofulous; having struma; a tendency to swelling of the glands in various parts of the body.

Stye. An inflamed tumour on the edge of the eyelid. Hordeolum. Subcutaneous. Situated under the skin.

Sub-paralytic. Somewhat paralysed; a not clearly defined effect of paralysis.

Sulphate. A salt formed by the union of sulphuric acid, composed of hydrogen, sulphur, and oxygen in these proportions, ($H_2 S O_4$), with a base or elementary substance, such as lime, potassium, or sodium, &c.

Sulphur. Brimstone; one of the elementary substances.

Sulphuric acid. An acid composed of one equivalent of sulphur, two of hydrogen, and four of oxygen ($Ha S O_4$).

Suppurating. Mattering, festering; accumulating of pus, yellow matter.

Suppuration. Formation of pus; process of producing purulent, corrupt matter.

Sycosis. A tubercular eruption upon the scalp or bearded part of the face; chin-welk.

Sympathetic. Dependent on sympathy or irritation.

Sympathetic nerve. It consists of nerves having one or more ganglia, which are nucleated nerve cells, and centres of nerve power to the fibres connected with them.

Sympathetic nerve system. A secondary nervous system, supposed to control the involuntary muscles and processes of alimentation or nutrition, a fact now generally accepted.

Symptom. A sign of disease or phenomenon which indicates disease, and especially the kind of disease.

Symptomatology, A treatise on the symptoms of disease.

Synovia. A lubricating fluid, secreted at the joints of the bones; hence synovial.

Synovitis. Inflammation of synovial membrane of the joint.

Synthetic. Pertaining to synthesis, or the uniting or building up of elements into a compound; the reverse of analysis.

Syphilis. The venereal disease; a virulent and specific disease, the result of contagion.

T

Tabes A wasting away; atrophy; emaciation.

Tenalgia crepitans. Crackling of the sinews.

Tendons. Fibrous cords attached to the extremities of certain muscles, and attaching them to the body or other firm textures.

Tentacle. A handle, or filiform process of insectivorous plants; also found in animals for the purpose of prehension, touch; for example, the feelers of a snail.

Tetanus, Tonic spasms. A spasmodic contraction of the muscles of voluntary motion with tension, rigidity, and stiffness.

Therapeutics. That branch of pathology which has for its object the treatment and cure of disease.

Thorax. That part of the human trunk, situated between the neck and the abdomen, containing the heart, &c. ; the cavity of the chest.

Tinnitus aurium. Ringing in the ears; often merely imaginary, or the result of indigestion; sometimes indicative of brain or functional disturbance of the heart; or it may be connected with deafness.

Tissue. The texture or minute structure of which organs are composed.

Tissues. Animal, divisible, according to Virchow and others, into three groups. These are: I. Cellular tissues, exclusively consisting of cells, such as the skin, nails, &c. II. Intercellular tissues, in which one cell is regularly separated from the others by intermediate or intercellular substance, such as connective-tissues, &c III. Various tissues, in which the cells have attained specific higher forms of development, such as nerves, &c. Virchow also places blood with its blood cells or corpuscles into this group.

Tissue salts. See Cell salts.

Tonic. A medicine that increases the strength, and gives vigour of action to the system.

Tonsils. Two oblong glands situated on each side of the fauces at the root of the tongue.

Tonsilitis. Inflammation of the tonsils; a form of sore throat.

Torpid. Having lost the power of exertion and feeling, or of muscular action.'

Torpor. Inactivity; loss of motion.

Trachea. The windpipe.

Transosmose. The passing of a fluid through a porous body, such as the products of chemical change through the porous porcelain jar of a Bunsen's battery; or the nutritive components of the blood through the walls of the blood-vessels at certain parts of the body.

Transude. To pass through the pores.

Triturate. To rub or grind to a very fine powder.

Tubercle. A small swelling or tumour on animal bodies, of the size of a hemp seed or of a pea, having a tendency to caseous or callcareous deposit; hence tubercular disease of the lungs.

Tumour. A swelling; a morbid enlargement.

Tunic. A membrane that covers some organ.

Tympanitis. A flatulent distension of the abdomen.

Typhoid or Enteric fever. A lingering fever, with great prostration, langour, stupor, in which the bowels are implicated.

Typhoid. Resembling typhus.

U

Ulcers. Sores on any part of the body discharging morbid matter.

Umbilicus. The navel; hence umbilical.

Urea. A crystalline substance obtained from urine.

Uric acid. A white tasteless and inodorous acid, contained in urine.

Urine. An animal fluid secreted by the kidneys, from whence it is conveyed to the bladder by the ureters, and discharged through the urethra.

Uterine. Pertaining to the uterus, or womb.

Uterus. Womb.

Uvula. A small nipple-like body or projection drooping from the middle of the arch of the palate.

V

Vaccination. The act of innoculating with the cow-pox.

Vaginal. Resembling a sheath; pertaining to the vagina, the canal. which leads from the external orifice to the uterus.

Vaginismus. Congestion or inflammation of the vagina.

Varicose. Preternaturally enlarged or dilated, as applied to the veins.

Variola. Small-pox.

Vascular. Full of blood vessels.

Vaseline. Obtained from petroleum, used as an ointment.

Vaso-motor. That which gives motion in the veins, &c.

Veins. Vessels in the animal body, which receive the blood from the extreme arteries through the capillaries, and return it to the auricles of the heart.

Vermicular. Resembling the motion of a worm.

Vertebræ. The individual bones forming the back-bone or spine.

Vertebrated. Having a spine with joints; a back-bone containing the spinal marrow.

Vertigo. Giddiness ; dizziness, or swimming of the head.

Vesicle. A little bladder, or a portion of the cuticle separated from the skin, and filled with fluid.

Villi. Minute thread-like projections, like velvet pile, on the mucous -lining of the smaller intestine for the purpose of absorption.

Viscera. Internal organs, as the contents of the thoracic and abdominal cavities.

Vitreous humour. A pellucid (clear, transparent) delicate jelly, which. fills the bulb of the eye behind the crystalline lens.

Volatilise. To cause a substance to pass off by evaporation.

W

Warts. Hard excrescences on the skin.

Whitlow. Inflammation about the root of a nail, commonly terminating in suppuration.

Y

Yolk-fat. The oil found in minute globules along with the yolk of an egg, containing phosphorus.

THE REFERENCE TABLE AND GENERAL INDEX.

IN this Reference Table **numbers only** are appended to each disease for the sake of brevity. They refer to the twelve sections of the Therapeutical Index, and represent the remedies from No. 1 to No.12 in the numerical order in which they are arranged, as seen on page 125. These numbers show *which* remedies may have to be given in the different ailments, and must be looked up under the *corresponding number* in the Therapeutical Index as to *when* and for which special symptoms they ought to be given. For the special reasons *why,* see DR. SCHÜSSLER'S explanations referred to in the pages indicated. A careful study of the "Characteristics" in the early part of the book, and of each section in the Therapeutical Index, will familiarize with the leading symptoms of a disease, and the range of action of each of the cell salts. It is hoped this will form a Key to a correct selection of the required remedies for the treatment of the various diseases and their characteristic symptoms. Many diseases are found to pass through three evolutions or stages. With the appropriate cell salts, the intensity and duration of the malady in each stage can be greatly reduced, as may be noticed in inflammation of the lungs, etc., and health soon restored. If the treatment of first stages be prompt, second and third stages may often be prevented, and the disease thus cut short, and suffering averted. Cases often become chronic and sometimes very tedious; not so here, where Nature is supplied with the natural substances and direct means of repair for the cells of the blood or of the tissues. In cases where the *mucous membrane or linings* are affected, the characteristics of the secretions or discharges may be very various in colour or consistency, which explains the great number of remedies after such ailments.

The Dose, the *Time* of taking, and *Directions* for external applications, etc., will be found on page 125. In those aillments where *Ferric phosphate* is recommended, it may be given alternately with any of the remedies specified, as those ailments incline to have inflammatory, congestive, or febrile tendencies. When a person is not able to judge of the exact length of time a remedy should be taken for a certain stage or certain symptoms, and cannot decide between two remedies if there are symptoms for both, he need not hesitate, but give both alternately until one or other symptom subside, for which they are given.

DR. SCHÜSSLER wrote his Therapeutics for the use of medical men, and with their knowledge of symptoms and pathological conditions, without the aid of the Thereapeutical Index, they can get all information in the concisely written pages of the book itself. But for others, the extensions in the Therapeutical Index, with frequently repeated details, names of diseases, and characteristic symptoms, may be a help, as well as my alphabetical arrangement of the Reference Table.

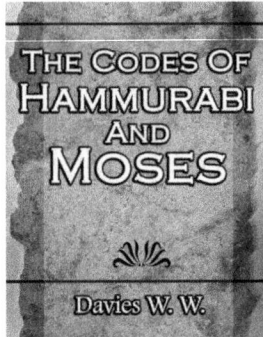

The Codes Of Hammurabi And Moses
W. W. Davies

QTY

The discovery of the Hammurabi Code is one of the greatest achievements of archaeology, and is of paramount interest, not only to the student of the Bible, but also to all those interested in ancient history...

Religion   **ISBN: *1-59462-338-4***   **Pages:132**
MSRP $12.95

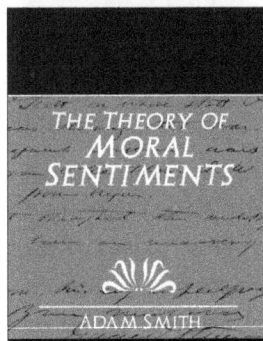

The Theory of Moral Sentiments
Adam Smith

QTY

This work from 1749. contains original theories of conscience amd moral judgment and it is the foundation for systemof morals.

Philosophy ISBN: *1-59462-777-0*   **Pages:536**
MSRP $19.95

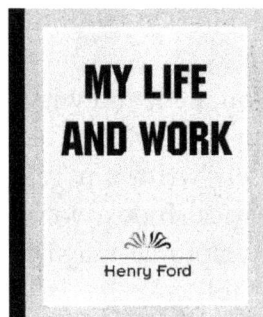

Jessica's First Prayer
Hesba Stretton

QTY

In a screened and secluded corner of one of the many railway-bridges which span the streets of London there could be seen a few years ago, from five o'clock every morning until half past eight, a tidily set-out coffee-stall, consisting of a trestle and board, upon which stood two large tin cans, with a small fire of charcoal burning under each so as to keep the coffee boiling during the early hours of the morning when the work-people were thronging into the city on their way to their daily toil...

Pages:84

Childrens   ISBN: *1-59462-373-2*   *MSRP $9.95*

My Life and Work
Henry Ford

QTY

Henry Ford revolutionized the world with his implementation of mass production for the Model T automobile. Gain valuable business insight into his life and work with his own auto-biography... "We have only started on our development of our country we have not as yet, with all our talk of wonderful progress, done more than scratch the surface. The progress has been wonderful enough but..."

Pages:300

Biographies/   ISBN: *1-59462-198-5*   *MSRP $21.95*

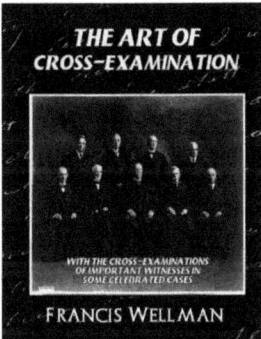

The Art of Cross-Examination
Francis Wellman

QTY

I presume it is the experience of every author, after his first book is published upon an important subject, to be almost overwhelmed with a wealth of ideas and illustrations which could readily have been included in his book, and which to his own mind, at least, seem to make a second edition inevitable. Such certainly was the case with me; and when the first edition had reached its sixth impression in five months, I rejoiced to learn that it seemed to my publishers that the book had met with a sufficiently favorable reception to justify a second and considerably enlarged edition. ..

Pages:412

Reference   ISBN: *1-59462-647-2*   *MSRP $19.95*

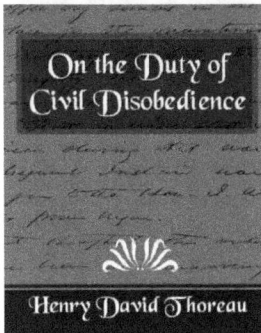

On the Duty of Civil Disobedience
Henry David Thoreau

QTY

Thoreau wrote his famous essay, On the Duty of Civil Disobedience, as a protest against an unjust but popular war and the immoral but popular institution of slave-owning. He did more than write—he declined to pay his taxes, and was hauled off to gaol in consequence. Who can say how much this refusal of his hastened the end of the war and of slavery ?

Law   ISBN: *1-59462-747-9*   **Pages:48**
                                         MSRP $7.45

Dream Psychology Psychoanalysis for Beginners
Sigmund Freud

QTY

Sigmund Freud, born Sigismund Schlomo Freud (May 6, 1856 - September 23, 1939), was a Jewish-Austrian neurologist and psychiatrist who co-founded the psychoanalytic school of psychology. Freud is best known for his theories of the unconscious mind, especially involving the mechanism of repression; his redefinition of sexual desire as mobile and directed towards a wide variety of objects; and his therapeutic techniques, especially his understanding of transference in the therapeutic relationship and the presumed value of dreams as sources of insight into unconscious desires.

Pages:196

Psychology   ISBN: *1-59462-905-6*   *MSRP $15.45*

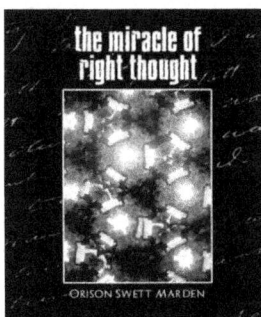

The Miracle of Right Thought
Orison Swett Marden

QTY

Believe with all of your heart that you will do what you were made to do. When the mind has once formed the habit of holding cheerful, happy, prosperous pictures, it will not be easy to form the opposite habit. It does not matter how improbable or how far away this realization may see, or how dark the prospects may be, if we visualize them as best we can, as vividly as possible, hold tenaciously to them and vigorously struggle to attain them, they will gradually become actualized, realized in the life. But a desire, a longing without endeavor, a yearning abandoned or held indifferently will vanish without realization.

Pages:360

Self Help   ISBN: *1-59462-644-8*   *MSRP $25.45*

QTY

The Rosicrucian Cosmo-Conception Mystic Christianity *by Max Heindel*　ISBN: *1-59462-188-8*　**$38.95**
The Rosicrucian Cosmo-conception is not dogmatic, neither does it appeal to any other authority than the reason of the student. It is: not controversial, but is: sent forth in the, hope that it may help to clear..　　New Age/Religion Pages 646

Abandonment To Divine Providence *by Jean-Pierre de Caussade*　ISBN: *1-59462-228-0*　**$25.95**
"The Rev. Jean Pierre de Caussade was one of the most remarkable spiritual writers of the Society of Jesus in France in the 18th Century. His death took place at Toulouse in 1751. His works have gone through many editions and have been republished...　Inspirational/Religion Pages 400

Mental Chemistry *by Charles Haanel*　ISBN: *1-59462-192-6*　**$23.95**
Mental Chemistry allows the change of material conditions by combining and appropriately utilizing the power of the mind. Much like applied chemistry creates something new and unique out of careful combinations of chemicals the mastery of mental chemistry...　New Age Pages 354

The Letters of Robert Browning and Elizabeth Barret Barrett 1845-1846 vol II　ISBN: *1-59462-193-4*　**$35.95**
by Robert Browning and Elizabeth Barrett
　　Biographies Pages 596

Gleanings In Genesis (volume I) *by Arthur W. Pink*　ISBN: *1-59462-130-6*　**$27.45**
Appropriately has Genesis been termed "the seed plot of the Bible" for in it we have, in germ form, almost all of the great doctrines which are afterwards fully developed in the books of Scripture which follow...　Religion/Inspirational Pages 420

The Master Key *by L. W. de Laurence*　ISBN: *1-59462-001-6*　**$30.95**
In no branch of human knowledge has there been a more lively increase of the spirit of research during the past few years than in the study of Psychology, Concentration and Mental Discipline. The requests for authentic lessons in Thought Control, Mental Discipline and...　New Age/Business Pages 422

The Lesser Key Of Solomon Goetia *by L. W. de Laurence*　ISBN: *1-59462-092-X*　**$9.95**
This translation of the first book of the "Lernegton" which is now for the first time made accessible to students of Talismanic Magic was done, after careful collation and edition, from numerous Ancient Manuscripts in Hebrew, Latin, and French...　New Age/Occult Pages 92

Rubaiyat Of Omar Khayyam *by Edward Fitzgerald*　ISBN:*1-59462-332-5*　**$13.95**
Edward Fitzgerald, whom the world has already learned, in spite of his own efforts to remain within the shadow of anonymity, to look upon as one of the rarest poets of the century, was born at Bredfield, in Suffolk, on the 31st of March, 1809. He was the third son of John Purcell...　Music Pages 172

Ancient Law *by Henry Maine*　ISBN: *1-59462-128-4*　**$29.95**
The chief object of the following pages is to indicate some of the earliest ideas of mankind, as they are reflected in Ancient Law, and to point out the relation of those ideas to modern thought.　Religion/History Pages 452

Far-Away Stories *by William J. Locke*　ISBN: *1-59462-129-2*　**$19.45**
"Good wine needs no bush, but a collection of mixed vintages does. And this book is just such a collection. Some of the stories I do not want to remain buried for ever in the museum files of dead magazine-numbers an author's not unpardonable vanity..."　Fiction Pages 272

Life of David Crockett *by David Crockett*　ISBN: *1-59462-250-7*　**$27.45**
"Colonel David Crockett was one of the most remarkable men of the times in which he lived. Born in humble life, but gifted with a strong will, an indomitable courage, and unremitting perseverance...　Biographies/New Age Pages 424

Lip-Reading *by Edward Nitchie*　ISBN: *1-59462-206-X*　**$25.95**
Edward B. Nitchie, founder of the New York School for the Hard of Hearing, now the Nitchie School of Lip-Reading, Inc, wrote "LIP-READING Principles and Practice". The development and perfecting of this meritorious work on lip-reading was an undertaking...　How-to Pages 400

A Handbook of Suggestive Therapeutics, Applied Hypnotism, Psychic Science　ISBN: *1-59462-214-0*　**$24.95**
by Henry Munro
　Health/New Age/Health/Self-help Pages 376

A Doll's House: and Two Other Plays *by Henrik Ibsen*　ISBN: *1-59462-112-8*　**$19.95**
Henrik Ibsen created this classic when in revolutionary 1848 Rome. Introducing some striking concepts in playwriting for the realist genre, this play has been studied the world over.　Fiction/Classics/Plays 308

The Light of Asia *by sir Edwin Arnold*　ISBN: *1-59462-204-3*　**$13.95**
In this poetic masterpiece, Edwin Arnold describes the life and teachings of Buddha. The man who was to become known as Buddha to the world was born as Prince Gautama of India but he rejected the worldly riches and abandoned the reigns of power when...　Religion/History/Biographies Pages 170

The Complete Works of Guy de Maupassant *by Guy de Maupassant*　ISBN: *1-59462-157-8*　**$16.95**
"For days and days, nights and nights, I had dreamed of that first kiss which was to consecrate our engagement, and I knew not on what spot I should put my lips..."　Fiction/Classics Pages 240

The Art of Cross-Examination *by Francis L. Wellman*　ISBN: *1-59462-309-0*　**$26.95**
Written by a renowned trial lawyer, Wellman imparts his experience and uses case studies to explain how to use psychology to extract desired information through questioning.　How-to/Science/Reference Pages 408

Answered or Unanswered? *by Louisa Vaughan*　ISBN: *1-59462-248-5*　**$10.95**
Miracles of Faith in China
　　Religion Pages 112

The Edinburgh Lectures on Mental Science (1909) *by Thomas*　ISBN: *1-59462-008-3*　**$11.95**
This book contains the substance of a course of lectures recently given by the writer in the Queen Street Hall, Edinburgh. Its purpose is to indicate the Natural Principles governing the relation between Mental Action and Material Conditions...　New Age/Psychology Pages 148

Ayesha *by H. Rider Haggard*　ISBN: *1-59462-301-5*　**$24.95**
Verily and indeed it is the unexpected that happens! Probably if there was one person upon the earth from whom the Editor of this, and of a certain previous history, did not expect to hear again...　Classics Pages 380

Ayala's Angel *by Anthony Trollope*　ISBN: *1-59462-352-X*　**$29.95**
The two girls were both pretty, but Lucy who was twenty-one who supposed to be simple and comparatively unattractive, whereas Ayala was credited, as her Bombwhat romantic name might show, with poetic charm and a taste for romance. Ayala when her father died was nineteen...　Fiction Pages 484

The American Commonwealth *by James Bryce*　ISBN: *1-59462-286-8*　**$34.45**
An interpretation of American democratic political theory. It examines political mechanics and society from the perspective of Scotsman James Bryce　Politics Pages 572

Stories of the Pilgrims *by Margaret P. Pumphrey*　ISBN: *1-59462-116-0*　**$17.95**
This book explores pilgrims religious oppression in England as well as their escape to Holland and eventual crossing to America on the Mayflower, and their early days in New England...　History Pages 268

QTY

The Fasting Cure *by Sinclair Upton*   ISBN: *1-59462-222-1* **$13.95**
*In the Cosmopolitan Magazine for May, 1910, and in the Contemporary Review (London) for April, 1910, I published an article dealing with my experi-
ences in fasting. I have written a great many magazine articles, but never one which attracted so much attention... New Age/Self Help/Health Pages 164*

Hebrew Astrology *by Sepharial*   ISBN: *1-59462-308-2* **$13.45**
*In these days of advanced thinking it is a matter of common observation that we have left many of the old landmarks behind and that we are now pressing
forward to greater heights and to a wider horizon than that which represented the mind-content of our progenitors... Astrology Pages 144*

Thought Vibration or The Law of Attraction in the Thought World   ISBN: *1-59462-127-6* **$12.95**

by William Walker Atkinson   *Psychology/Religion Pages 144*

Optimism *by Helen Keller*   ISBN: *1-59462-108-X* **$15.95**
*Helen Keller was blind, deaf, and mute since 19 months old, yet famously learned how to overcome these handicaps, communicate with the world, and
spread her lectures promoting optimism. An inspiring read for everyone... Biographies/Inspirational Pages 84*

Sara Crewe *by Frances Burnett*   ISBN: *1-59462-360-0* **$9.45**
*In the first place, Miss Minchin lived in London. Her home was a large, dull, tall one, in a large, dull square, where all the houses were alike, and all the
sparrows were alike, and where all the door-knockers made the same heavy sound... Childrens/Classic Pages 88*

The Autobiography of Benjamin Franklin *by Benjamin Franklin*   ISBN: *1-59462-135-7* **$24.95**
*The Autobiography of Benjamin Franklin has probably been more extensively read than any other American historical work, and no other book of its kind
has had such ups and downs of fortune. Franklin lived for many years in England, where he was agent... Biographies/History Pages 332*

Name	
Email	
Telephone	
Address	
City, State ZIP	

☐ **Credit Card**   ☐ **Check / Money Order**

Credit Card Number	
Expiration Date	
Signature	

*Please Mail to: Book Jungle
PO Box 2226
Champaign, IL 61825
or Fax to: 630-214-0564*

ORDERING INFORMATION

web: *www.bookjungle.com*
email: *sales@bookjungle.com*
fax: *630-214-0564*
mail: *Book Jungle PO Box 2226 Champaign, IL 61825*
or PayPal *to sales@bookjungle.com*

Please contact us for bulk discounts

DIRECT-ORDER TERMS

**20% Discount if You Order
Two or More Books**
Free Domestic Shipping!
Accepted: Master Card, Visa,
Discover, American Express

www.ingramcontent.com/pod-product-compliance
Lightning Source LLC
Chambersburg PA
CBHW080531090426
42733CB00015B/2557